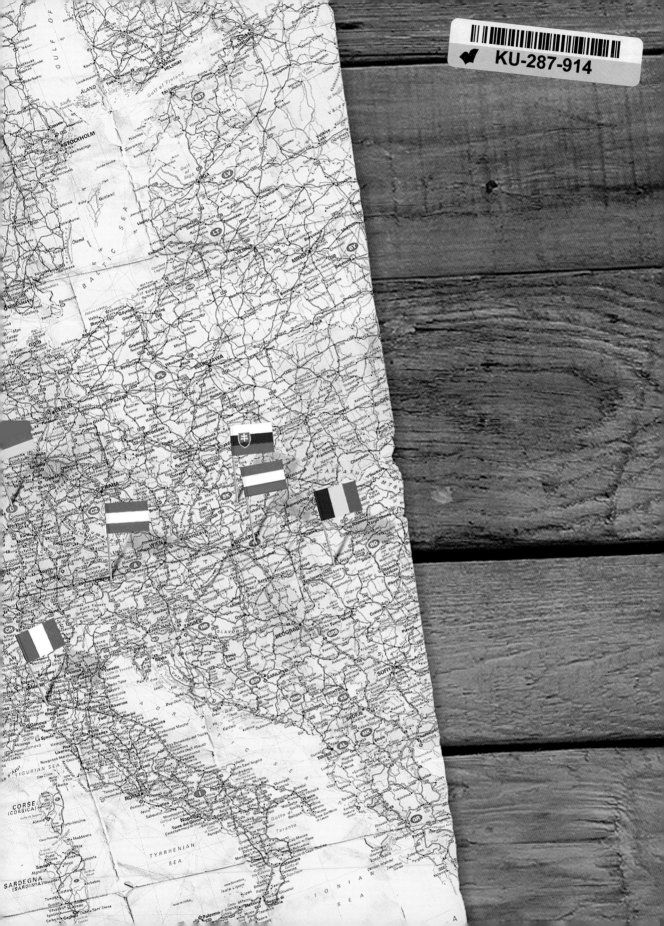

THE HAIRY BIKERS'
BIG BOOK OF
BAKING

THE HAIRY BIKERS'
BIG BOOK OF
BAKING

WEIDENFELD & NICOLSON

We'd like to dedicate this book to Nicola, Natalie, Holly and all at James Grant Management with thanks for everything you've done for us.

First published in hardback in Great Britain in 2012 by
Weidenfeld & Nicolson, an imprint of the Orion Publishing Group Ltd
Orion House, 5 Upper St Martin's Lane, London WC2H 9EA
an Hachette UK Company

Food photography: Cristian Barnett
Location photography: Cristian Barnett and Sammy-Jo Squire
Food stylist: Sammy-Jo Squire
Prop stylist: Guiliana Casarotti
Designer: Kate Barr
Editor: Jinny Johnson
Proofreader: Elise See Tai
Indexer: Cherry Ekins
Photographer's assistant: Roy Baron
Food stylist's assistants: Becca Watson and Nikki Morgan

Printed and bound in China

The Orion Publishing Group's policy is to use papers that are natural, renewable and recyclable and made from wood grown in sustainable forests. The logging and manufacturing processes are expected to conform to the environmental regulations of the country of origin.

www.orionbooks.co.uk

OUR EUROPEAN BAKEATION

There's a magic about baking. Like a wizard, you assemble the ingredients for your spell and put things together. The potion doesn't look like much when it goes into the oven but when it comes out, it's turned into a fabulous golden loaf or a yummy spongy cake. Kitchen alchemy!

Ever since we were nippers, we've loved baking and our passion has got stronger over the years. A while back, we did our 'Hairy Bakers' series on baking in Britain and it became one of our most successful ever. But we're nosy beggars and we've always wanted to discover all the best baking recipes and not just from these shores. We've had a look at what goes on across the English Channel and we've brought back some cracking recipes for you!

Our 'Bakeation' – our big bad summer holiday – took us on a four-month, 7,000-mile journey into the unknown territories of European baking. We ate our way through many countries and found that baking is not only alive and well, it's thriving. All over Europe we met people who put personality and passion into their baking. And we don't mean just cakes, breads and fancies. We ate whole baked meals, soufflés, pies, one-pot wonders, meatloaf – anything that goes into the oven to be transformed by heat. We found the best bread in Oslo, the finest patisseries in Vienna, the happiest food in Italy, the most heartfelt recipes in Romania, and a good laugh around every corner. We discovered oddities – like the Norwegians' love of cardamom, a spice brought back from Turkey by Viking travellers and traders, and we learned how this aromatic ingredient brings something so warming and delicious to their baking.

Many of these recipes are classics of their country and for some there are countless versions that claim to be the ultimate – wars are fought over such things! The recipes in this book are our take on these classics. We've cooked them all with a real sense of pride and satisfaction and we know they work for the British cook. Don't be put off by an unfamiliar name. Try these great recipes and take your taste buds off to France, Hungary or Spain via your oven – no passport required!

There's a joy in baking – a huge grin factor. We experienced it when we watched our mums baking when we were kids and we saw it again all over Europe. People bake for fun, for comfort, and there's nothing that shows love better than a home-made cake or a loaf of bread still warm from the oven. We've been given lots of secrets by the fantastic bakers we met and now we want to share them with you. Food can be the best holiday souvenir – tans and memories fade but a recipe is there for life. Get out your wooden spoons and have some fun.

Discover that magic in your own kitchen and bake something delicious today!

NORWAY

This was our first visit
to Norway and it's a
wonderfully fresh, clean
healthy place. Fantastic
food, especially the bread
— which is Viking good!
— and some surprises
to be tried, like savoury
cheesecake and spicy
cardamom cake.

JARLSBERG TWIST BREAD
(Jarlsberg vri brød)

———

Makes 4 small loaves

We love this soft, moist bread which tastes great just as it is or can be split and filled with your favourite sandwich fillings. Jarlsberg is Norway's best known cheese and has a deliciously sweet, nutty flavour. A guilty pleasure for everyone – not just Vikings.

1 x 7g sachet of fast-action dried yeast	100ml whole milk
1 tbsp caster sugar	50g butter, cut into cubes
250ml warm water	1 medium egg, beaten
500g plain flour, plus extra for dusting	sunflower oil, for greasing
275g Jarlsberg cheese, grated	3 tbsp finely chopped parsley
2 tsp fine sea salt	

Put the yeast and sugar in a medium bowl, add 125ml of the warm water and whisk well. Set aside in a warm place for about 10 minutes or until you can see a light, beige froth floating on the surface of the mixture. Mix the flour, 100g of the cheese and the salt in a large bowl and make a well in the centre. Set aside the remaining cheese until later.

Pour the milk into a saucepan, add the remaining 125ml of water and the butter. Place over a low heat for just a few seconds until the liquid is lukewarm and the butter has melted. Don't let the mixture overheat. Stir the warm buttered milk and the egg into the yeast mixture. Gradually stir it all into the flour with a wooden spoon and then mix with your hands until everything comes together to form a soft, spongy dough.

Turn the dough out on to a lightly floured surface and knead for about 5 minutes until smooth and elastic. Put the dough in a large, lightly oiled bowl and cover loosely with oiled clingfilm. Leave the dough to rise in a warm place for about 40 minutes or until it has doubled in size.

Return the dough to a floured surface and knock it back with your knuckles before kneading for a minute. Divide the dough into 4 balls and roll each ball into a rectangle measuring 25 x 20cm. Mix the remaining 175g of cheese with the parsley and sprinkle over the dough rectangles, leaving a 1cm gap around the edges. Beginning with the short ends, roll up the rectangles tightly like Swiss rolls and squeeze the ends to seal.

Place 1 of the dough rolls vertically in front of you and cut through the centre up to about 5mm from the top. Twist each half of the dough over the other to form a braid, leaving the open sides, revealing the cheese and parsley, on top if possible. Repeat with the other pieces of dough.

Carefully transfer the loaves to a large baking sheet lined with baking parchment. Space them well apart and tuck in the ends neatly to preserve the twisted shape. Leave to rise for 30 minutes or until doubled in size. Preheat the oven to 200°C/Fan 180°C/Gas 6. Bake the loaves in the centre of the oven for 35–40 minutes or until well risen and golden brown. The bases should sound hollow when tapped. Leave to cool for 10 minutes before serving.

SAVOURY PIES WITH JARLSBERG CHEESE & HAM

Every country has something like these little pies – Polish pierogi, Indian samosas, Spanish and Argentinian empanadas – and this is Norway's version, made with Jarlsberg cheese and caraway seeds for that special Norwegian flavour. We give these dix points! If you're a lazybones you could use puff pastry, but you'll end up with something that's more like a fried pasty. Try these as a great little starter or beer blotter.

DOUGH	FILLING
700ml lukewarm water	2 tbsp olive oil
1 tbsp sugar	1 onion, finely chopped
1½ tbsp fast-action dried yeast	2 garlic cloves, crushed
950g flour, plus extra for dusting	200g boiled, smoked ham
225ml whole milk	100g Jarlsberg cheese, grated
2 tsp salt	1 tbsp finely chopped parsley
70g butter	1 tsp caraway seeds
2 eggs	flaked sea salt
1 tbsp oil, for greasing the tray	freshly ground black pepper
1 egg, beaten, for glazing and sealing	

First make your starter mixture for the dough. Pour the lukewarm water into a bowl, add the sugar and yeast, then stir in 150g of the flour. Add a quarter of the rest of the flour, mix well and leave the mixture to rise for 2–3 hours.

Add the milk, salt, the rest of the flour and the butter and eggs, then knead the mixture into a relatively firm dough. Leave it to rise for 2 hours.

Meanwhile, make the filling. Heat the olive oil in a frying pan, add the onion and cook gently for about 5 minutes until transparent. Add the garlic and continue to cook for another 2 minutes. Stir in the ham, cheese, parsley and caraway seeds, then season to taste and set aside to cool.

Roll out the dough thinly on a floured surface and cut out 12 small circles. Use a glass if you don't have a pastry cutter. Place a spoonful of filling on to one half of a pastry circle, then brush the edges with the beaten egg, and fold the pastry over to enclose the filling. Squeeze the edges together and brush again with the beaten egg. Fill the rest of the circles in the same way. Preheat the oven to 200°C/Fan 180°C/Gas 6.

Place the pies on a greased baking tray and bake them for 12–15 minutes until golden.

SCANDINAVIAN RYE BREAD
(Rugbrød)

Norwegians love their bread and loaves made with rye flour are particularly popular. This wonderful bread tastes a bit like sourdough – only better. We like it made with a mixture of white flour and rye so it isn't too heavy, but you can change the proportions if you prefer a darker loaf – you may need to add extra water if using more rye. We cooked this by the side of a fjord after a trip on a longship, and we ate it with codfish soup.

175ml whole milk	200g strong white bread flour,
175ml water	plus extra for dusting
2 tbsp dark soft brown sugar	1 tbsp fine sea salt
1 x 7g sachet of fast-action dried yeast	2 tsp caraway seeds
250g rye flour	sunflower oil, for greasing

Put the milk, water and sugar in a small saucepan and heat very gently, stirring constantly, for just a few seconds until the liquid is lukewarm and the sugar has dissolved. Remove the pan from the heat and pour the mixture into a bowl. Stir in the yeast and leave for 10 minutes until there is a light froth floating on the surface.

Put all the flour, rye and white, in a large bowl, stir in the salt and caraway seeds, then make a well in the centre. Pour the warm yeast mixture on to the flour and mix with a wooden spoon and then your hands to form a soft, spongy dough.

Turn the dough out on to a well-floured surface and knead for 10 minutes or until it is smooth and elastic. Kneading this dough can be hard work so you'll need to roll up your sleeves and give it some welly. Put the dough in a large, lightly oiled bowl and cover loosely with oiled clingfilm. Leave to rise in a warm place for about 1½ hours or until it has doubled in size.

Put the dough on a floured work surface and knock it back with your knuckles, then knead for another minute. Shape the dough into a fat oval or round loaf, pulling the dough from the top and sides and tucking it underneath to make a neat shape.

Place the loaf on a baking tray lined with baking parchment and score the surface 4 times with a sharp knife. Cover it loosely with the oiled clingfilm and leave to prove for a further 40–50 minutes until it has doubled in size once more.

Preheat the oven to 180°C/Fan 160°C/Gas 4. Bake the loaf in the centre of the oven for 40 minutes or until it is well risen and the base sounds hollow when tapped sharply. Cool for at least 20 minutes before serving.

NORWEGIAN FLATBREADS
(Lefse)

Makes 14

A true taste of Norway, these are a great treat and are often served at Christmas and other holidays. They're made with cooked and creamed sweetened potatoes, but you could use leftover mash if you like, and you can fill your lefse with savoury or sweet mixtures; good with a breakfast fry-up or with jam for tea.

1kg floury potatoes, (King Edward or Maris Piper)
4 tbsp double cream
50g butter, cut into cubes
2 tbsp caster sugar
1 tsp fine sea salt
225–250g plain flour, plus plenty for dusting

sunflower oil, for frying
softened butter, for serving

CINNAMON SUGAR (optional)
½ tsp ground cinnamon
2 tbsp caster sugar

Peel the potatoes and cut them into even-sized chunks. Put them in a large pan and cover with cold water, then place over a high heat and bring to the boil. Reduce the heat slightly and simmer for 10–15 minutes until very tender. Drain the potatoes well in a colander, then tip them back into the pan. Place the pan over a low heat for a couple of minutes, stirring the potatoes every now and then to let as much steam and moisture as possible escape – the potatoes should break up as you stir. Mash them roughly with a potato masher.

Transfer the mash to a large bowl and, using an electric hand-whisk, beat in the cream, butter, sugar and salt, then mix until the potatoes are very smooth. Alternatively, you can put the potatoes in a food mixer with the other ingredients and beat until smooth, but do not use a food processor. Leave the mixture to cool, then cover the surface with clingfilm and chill in the fridge for several hours or overnight.

When you're ready to cook the flatbreads, stir 225g of the flour into the creamed potatoes to make a smooth, pliable dough. Add a little more flour if it is a still a bit sticky. Bring the dough together with your hands, then knead it lightly and form it into a ball. Divide the dough into 14 even-sized pieces and roll them into balls. Dust the work surface and rolling pin heavily with flour and roll out 1 of the balls into a very thin round, measuring about 23cm across. You'll need to lift the dough a few times, turning and sprinkling it with more flour as you roll it thinner.

Heat a large non-stick frying pan or griddle over a medium-high heat and add a teaspoon of oil. Wipe around the pan carefully with a thick wad of folded kitchen paper to grease. Lift the flatbread over the rolling pin and drop it gently into the pan. Cook for about 2 minutes on each side until lightly browned, flipping it with a palette knife or spatula.

While the flatbread is cooking, roll out another ball of the dough and cook in exactly the same way. Between each flatbread, you'll need to wipe away any burnt flour and re-grease the frying pan or griddle with oil. Stack up the flatbreads as they are cooked and keep them warm or serve them as soon as they are ready. Serve with softened butter and cinnamon sugar if you like.

NORWEGIAN-STYLE SAVOURY CHEESECAKE

Serves 8–10

Cheesecakes are not only for pudding. We ate something similar to this fab savoury version in Norway and we've come up with our own hearty recipe. Made with Jarlsberg cheese, dill and smoked salmon – one of the country's best-loved foods – this is the classic taste of Norway all in one dish.

sunflower oil, for greasing
500g full-fat soft cheese, such as Philadelphia
2 tbsp cornflour
3 large eggs
200g Jarlsberg cheese, coarsely grated
1 tbsp fresh lemon juice
finely grated zest of ½ lemon
3 tbsp finely chopped fresh dill
2 tbsp finely snipped chives
300ml soured cream

flaked sea salt
freshly ground black pepper

TOPPING
200ml crème fraiche
150g sliced smoked salmon
½ small red onion, very finely sliced
3–4 tbsp lumpfish caviar (from delis or
    the chiller cabinets in large supermarkets)
a small bunch of fresh dill

Preheat the oven to 180°C/Fan 160°C/Gas 4. Lightly grease a 23cm spring-clip cake tin and line the base with baking parchment.

Put the soft cheese in a large bowl and beat with an electric hand-whisk until smooth. Gradually whisk in the cornflour, then add the eggs, 1 at a time, beating well in between each addition. You'll find you need to stop beating every now and then to push the mixture down in the bowl with a rubber spatula.

Once all the eggs have been beaten into the mixture, add the grated cheese, lemon juice and zest, dill and chives. Season well with salt and lots of black pepper and stir until thoroughly combined. Fold in the soured cream and pour the mixture into the prepared tin. Bake the cheesecake for 50–60 minutes or until it is slightly puffed up, set and golden brown. Leave to cool completely in the tin for at least an hour and then chill for a further 3 hours or overnight.

When you're ready to serve, run a knife around the edge of the cheesecake and take it out of the tin, peeling off the lining paper if it sticks. Transfer the cheesecake carefully to a large serving plate or board.

Spoon the crème fraiche over the surface of the cheesecake, and spread it over evenly with the back of the spoon, taking it right to the edge. Tear the smoked salmon into strips and arrange them loosely on top. Scatter over the sliced onion and dot with the lumpfish caviar, then garnish with little sprigs of dill. Season with more black pepper and take the cheesecake to the table.

SCANDINAVIAN TEA RING

Serves 12

This fantastic teatime treat tastes as good as it looks, and is packed full of nuts and dried fruit. It might look like a lot of work but it's all very easy, so give it a go and you'll thank us. Forget Danish pastries and start making this tea ring instead.

175ml whole milk
65g butter, softened
50g granulated sugar
1 x 7g sachet of fast-action dried yeast
375–400g plain flour, plus extra for dusting
½ tsp fine sea salt
2 tsp ground cardamom, ideally from seeds freshly ground in a pestle and mortar
1 medium egg, lightly beaten
sunflower oil, for greasing

FILLING
100g butter, softened
100g granulated sugar
2 tsp ground cinnamon

100g cut mixed candied peel
50g ground almonds
50g flaked almonds
50g glacé cherries (preferably undyed), cut into quarters

GLAZE
1 medium egg, beaten

DECORATION
125g icing sugar
5–6 tsp whole milk
4 glacé cherries (preferably undyed), quartered
5–10g flaked almonds (choose the most perfect ones)

Put the milk, butter and sugar in a small saucepan over a very low heat for a few seconds until just warm. Remove the pan from the heat and stir until the sugar dissolves. Don't allow the milk to overheat or the yeast won't work. Sprinkle the yeast over the milk mixture and stir, then leave for 10 minutes until a light foam forms on the surface.

Combine the flour, salt and cardamom in a large bowl until evenly mixed and make a well in the centre. Stir the beaten egg into the warm milk and then slowly pour the liquid on to the flour, mixing it with a wooden spoon and then your hands to form a soft, spongy dough.

Turn the dough out on to a well-floured surface and knead it for about 5 minutes until smooth and pliable. If the dough is too sticky to work with, add an extra 25g or so of flour.

Shape the dough into a ball and place it in a lightly oiled bowl. Cover with oiled clingfilm and leave to rise in a warm place for 1–1¼ hours or until it has doubled in size.

To make the filling, cream the butter, sugar and cinnamon together until light and fluffy. Stir in the candied peel, ground almonds, flaked almonds and cherries.

Return the dough to a floured work surface and knock it back with your knuckles before kneading it for another minute. Using a rolling pin, roll the dough into a neat 25 x 45cm rectangle. Spread the filling mixture evenly over the dough with a spatula or palette knife, leaving a 5mm border around the sides.

Roll the dough up firmly from one of the short ends – like a Swiss roll. Place the roll, with the joined side down, on a large baking tray lined with baking parchment. Brush one end lightly with the beaten egg and bring both ends together to make a ring shape. Press the ends gently together to seal.

Using kitchen scissors or a sharp knife, snip through the dough about 12 times, cutting halfway through to the centre (have a look at the picture on the next page). The cuts should be roughly every 4cm so that they look like the spokes of a cog. Make sure the join between the ends is correctly spaced within the cuts. Tease open each cut slightly to reveal the filling. Cover the ring loosely with oiled clingfilm and leave to rise for a further 40 minutes or until it has doubled in size once more.

Preheat the oven to 190°C/Fan 170°C/Gas 5. Brush the tea ring all over with the beaten egg to glaze. Bake for about 25 minutes or until well risen and deep golden brown, then remove from the oven and leave to cool on the baking tray.

To make the icing, sift the icing sugar into a bowl and stir in enough milk to give a smooth, pourable icing. Don't allow it to become too thin as the icing needs to sit on the tea ring without sliding off.

Transfer the tea ring to a serving plate or cake stand. Drizzle the icing slowly over the ring, allowing it to dribble down the sides. Leave for 5 minutes, then decorate with the quartered cherries and flaked almonds. Allow the icing to set for at least 30 minutes before serving.

POOR MAN'S COOKIES
(Fattigman)

Makes loads

At the posh end of Norwegian cookie making are the stamped cardamom cookies, also called goro, or affluent cookies, which you need a fancy press for. Fattigman are the poor relations, the poor man's cookies, but like lots of humble food they are well tasty. Strictly speaking, these don't belong here because they're not baked, but we wanted to include them as well as the posh version. You can get a fattigman cutter on the internet or simply cut the cookies into diamond shapes.

5 tbsp double cream	1 egg white
300g plain flour	5 egg yolks
½ tsp baking powder	5 tbsp caster sugar
½ tsp salt	1 tbsp brandy
½ tsp cinnamon	vegetable oil, for deep-frying
6 cardamom pods, split and the seeds ground to a powder	caster sugar, for sprinkling

Put the cream in a bowl and whip until it forms stiff peaks. In a separate bowl, sieve together the flour, baking powder, salt, cinnamon, and cardamom.

In another bowl, beat the egg white with an electric hand-whisk until stiff, then in yet another bowl beat the egg yolks with the sugar. Add the brandy to the egg yolk mixture, then stir in the cream and fold in the egg white. Add enough of the flour and spice mixture to make a dough. You may not need it all and if you do have any left, save it to dust the work surface when you roll out the dough. Leave the dough to rest in the fridge overnight if you can, or for at least an hour.

Dust the work surface with any leftover flour or some extra flour if necessary. Roll out the dough thinly and cut out cookies with your fattigman cutter if you have one. Alternatively, cut out diamond shapes measuring about 6cm long by 3cm wide. Make a little cut in the centre of each diamond, then tuck through one of the long points to form a little knot.

Heat the oil in a deep-fat fryer or a large saucepan to a moderate rumble – about 160°C. Fry the cookies a few at a time until golden, then remove and leave to drain and cool on kitchen paper. Sprinkle with sugar and enjoy with a cup of tea.

CARDAMOM COFFEE CAKE
(Kardemummakaka)

Makes 20 squares

There's no coffee in this, we can hear you shout! Well, you know what – this cake isn't called coffee cake because it contains coffee but because it's served at coffee time! It's very light, with a gentle cardamom flavour and a delicious crunchy almond topping.

200g butter, plus extra for greasing
2 tbsp cardamom pods
225g caster sugar
3 large eggs
300g self-raising flour

1 tsp baking powder
200ml semi-skimmed milk
3 heaped tbsp demerara sugar
40g flaked almonds

Preheat the oven to 190°C/Fan 170°C/Gas 5. Grease a 20 x 30cm cake or brownie tin and line it with baking parchment. Put the butter in a saucepan and melt it slowly, then remove the pan from the heat and leave the butter to cool.

Break open the cardamom pods and remove the seeds. Put the seeds in a pestle and mortar and pound them into a powder. You should end up with about 2 teaspoons. Set this aside.

Put the sugar and eggs in a large bowl and beat with an electric hand-whisk until pale and light. Add the cardamom, flour, baking powder, cooled melted butter and a little of the milk, then whisk until just combined.

Gradually add the rest of the milk, whisking constantly until the batter is smooth and has the texture of double cream. Pour into the prepared tin.

Mix together the demerara sugar and almonds and sprinkle the mixture over the top of the cake. Bake the cake in the centre of the oven for 30–35 minutes or until it's well risen and golden brown. Check by putting a skewer into the centre – it should come out clean, but if not, cook the cake for a little longer.

Leave the cake to cool in the tin for about 30 minutes, then cut it into squares before serving. If you'd like to serve the cake warm, remove it from the tin after 5 minutes of cooling.

NORWEGIAN ALMOND BARS

Makes at least 8

This recipe might sound a bit strange, but it is well worth a go and no one will guess you have used up some leftover mashed potato in the almond filling. The jam is our special touch that turns this into a supercharged Norwegian bakewell.

400g plain flour, sifted, plus extra for dusting
1 tsp baking powder
1 tsp salt
150g caster sugar
150g unsalted butter, cut into cubes, plus extra for greasing the baking tray
2 tbsp jam, cloudberry would be great, but raspberry will do

100g cold mashed potato
250g icing sugar
300g ground almonds
1 tsp cinnamon
6 cardamom pods, split and the seeds ground to a powder
1 tbsp water
1 egg white
1 egg yolk

You'll need a shallow baking tray, with sides, measuring about 25 x 30cm. Grease the tray and line the base with silicone paper. Preheat the oven to 200°C/Fan 180°C/Gas 6.

To make the biscuit base, mix the flour, baking powder, salt and sugar in a bowl. Add the cubes of butter and rub them into the dry ingredients with your fingertips until the mixture looks like gravel. Press about three-quarters of the biscuit mixture on to the base and set aside the rest for later. Place the tray in the oven and bake for about 10 minutes so that the base is partly cooked. Leave to cool slightly, then spread a layer of jam over the biscuit base. Keep the oven on.

Put the mashed potato, icing sugar, ground almonds, cinnamon, cardamom, water and egg white into a clean bowl and mix them together thoroughly. Spread this mixture over the jam on the biscuit base.

Take the remaining biscuit mixture and mix in the egg yolk to make a dough. Place this on a floured surface and roll it out into a rectangle. Cut the dough into strips and arrange them in a criss-cross lattice pattern on top of the filling.

Put the baking tray back in the oven and bake for 20–25 minutes until the lattice strips are cooked through and golden. Cool, then cut into bars and enjoy with a cup of coffee.

CARDAMOM & LEMON
STAMPED COOKIES

Makes 24

We discovered that cardamom is a really popular spice in Norway, used in many cake and biscuit recipes. Some say the spice was first brought back to the country hundreds of years ago by Vikings who worked as mercenaries in what was then Constantinople (now Istanbul). Whatever the truth, Norwegians are certainly keen on their cardamom. We made these cookies on a boat on the Geiranger Fjord – a stunning spot.

225g butter, softened
150g caster sugar
finely grated zest of 1 lemon
250g plain flour

100g ground almonds
3 tsp ground cardamom or 1 heaped tsp cardamom seeds, ground in a pestle and mortar

Preheat the oven to 190°C/Fan 170°C/Gas 5. Line 2 large baking trays with baking parchment.

Using an electric hand-whisk, beat the butter, sugar and lemon zest together in a large bowl until pale and fluffy. Beat in the flour, almonds and cardamom until the mixture is well combined and comes together to form a stiff dough.

Roll the dough into 24 balls and place 12 on each baking tray – make sure you leave space between each one. Press each cookie with a cookie stamp or the bottom of a glass to flatten and leave decorative indentations in the dough.

Bake a tray at a time for 12–14 minutes until the cookies are pale golden brown. Leave them to cool on the tray for a few minutes, then transfer to a wire rack. They will crisp up as they cool. Store the cookies in an airtight tin and eat within 7 days.

Tip: You can also make these cookies using a biscuit press. They'll be about half the size, so cook them for 10–12 minutes instead.

NIKKA'S NORWEGIAN BAKELSE

————

Makes about 8

We were shown how to make these by a lovely lady called Nikka, who's 94 years old and still baking. This is her recipe. Traditionally, you would cook these on a Norwegian bakelse iron, which produces very thin pancakes cooked from both sides simultaneously, but Nikka says you can use two cast-iron frying pans – one with a very clean bottom!

600g plain flour	30ml whipping cream
4 tbsp sugar	4 tbsp soured cream
½ tsp salt	5 tbsp melted butter, plus extra for greasing
1 large egg	1 litre cold water jam, for serving

Mix the flour, sugar and salt in a large bowl. In a jug, mix together the egg, whipping cream, soured cream, melted butter and half the water, then whisk until everything is fully combined.

Make a well in the dry ingredients and add the liquid. Using an electric hand-whisk, beat the mixture until it comes together as a smooth batter. It should be the consistency of thick pouring cream, but if not, then whisk in a little more of the cold water until it is.

Unless you have a Norwegian bakelse iron, get your frying pans ready and heat both over a medium heat. Brush some melted butter on to one of the frying pans and then ladle in some of the batter. Use enough batter to make a pancake of similar thickness to a French crêpe. Roll the batter around in the pan so that it covers the surface, then quickly brush the underside of the second cast-iron pan (the one the with clean bottom) with butter and place it on top of the cooking pancake. It should take about 2 minutes to cook.

Once the pancake is slightly browned and crisp, slide it out of the pan on to a plate. Keep going until the batter is used up. These are delicious spread with jam.

LOW COUNTRIES

It's not all cheese and windmills in these lands. There's loads of great baking to be found and lashings of luscious treats, such as chocolate truffle cake and a mega pork pie.

AMSTERDAM CARAMEL COOKIES
(*Koggetjes*)

Makes 15

These cookies are amazing. The story is that they were first baked in 1935 when their creator entered them in a cookery competition to find a true Amsterdam cookie. They were named after Dutch ships called 'kogge', which appear on the city's official seal.

125g butter, softened	**CARAMEL**
150g caster sugar	50g caster sugar
150g plain flour	1 tbsp water
½ tsp baking powder	

To make the caramel, put the sugar and water in a small saucepan and place over a low heat for 1–2 minutes until the sugar has dissolved, stirring occasionally. Turn up the heat and bring the syrup to a fast simmer, then cook without stirring for 5–8 minutes or until the sugar caramelises and turns a rich, golden brown. While the sugar is bubbling, line a small baking tray with baking parchment.

As soon as the sugar has caramelised, pour it on to the lined tray and allow it to spread. You may need to tilt the tin a little in order to get a nice, thin layer, but it doesn't matter what shape it is, as the caramel will be broken up later. Always be really careful when working with caramel as it is mind-bendingly hot. Don't even dream of touching or tasting it until it is completely cold. Set the caramel aside to cool and harden for at least 15 minutes.

Preheat the oven to 180°C/Fan 160°C/Gas 4. Put the butter and sugar in a large bowl and beat with a wooden spoon until light and creamy. Add the flour and baking powder and stir well until the mixture comes together and forms a ball – you may need to use your hands.

Remove the cold caramel from the baking parchment and break it into chunky pieces. Tip them into a pestle and mortar and bash away to break them into very small shards. Alternatively, put the bits of caramel in a sturdy mixing bowl and break them up gently with the end of a rolling pin. The shards don't have to be exactly the same size and don't grind them up too much. Pieces of about 3–5mm are about right.

Stir or knead the pieces of caramel into the biscuit dough until they are completely mixed through. Divide the dough into 15 even pieces and roll these into small balls. Place the balls on 2 large baking trays lined with baking parchment – space them well apart as they will spread as they cook. Flatten the cookies carefully so that they are about 1cm thick.

Bake the cookies, a tray at a time, for 10–12 minutes until they are pale golden brown and leave them to cool on the trays. The cookies will be soft when you take them out of the oven, but will crisp up as they cool. Store in an airtight tin and eat within 5 days.

LAZYBONES BUNS
(Luilakbollen)

—

Makes 8

Luilak is a Dutch festival held on the day before Whit Sunday. Young people start to crowd the streets at four in the morning, whistling, banging on doors and ringing bells to make as much noise as they can. Any young person who fails to get up is a 'lazybones'. As well as making lots of noise, the revellers stuff themselves with goodies, including these very tasty buns, which are a bit like our hot cross buns.

50g caster sugar	1 tsp ground cinnamon
50g butter, cut into cubes	finely grated zest of 1 lemon
150ml semi-skimmed milk	1 large egg, beaten
1 x 7g sachet of fast-action dried yeast	125g raisins or 100g raisins and 25g currants
375g strong white flour, plus extra for dusting	sunflower oil, for greasing
½ tsp fine sea salt	butter and syrup or honey, to serve

Put the sugar, butter and milk in a small saucepan and heat very gently for a few seconds until just warm. Take care that the milk doesn't get too hot or the yeast won't work. Pour the milk mixture into a heatproof bowl and stir in the yeast. Leave for 10 minutes or until a light foam forms on the surface.

Mix the flour, salt, cinnamon and lemon zest in a large bowl and make a well in the centre. Whisk the egg into the warm milk mixture, then pour it all on to the flour. Stir with a wooden spoon until the mixture forms a ball. Turn the mixture out on to a very lightly floured surface and knead for 5 minutes to make a smooth, pliable dough. Knead the fruit into the dough for a couple of minutes until it is evenly distributed. Place the dough in a lightly oiled bowl and cover with oiled clingfilm. Leave to rise in a warm place for 1½ hours, or until it has doubled in size and is spongy to touch.

Return the dough to the work surface and knock it back with your knuckles. Knead lightly, then divide the dough into 8 portions. Roll each of these into a ball, then pull the dough from around the sides and tuck it underneath the bun to give it a neat shape.

Place the buns on a large baking tray lined with baking parchment and flatten them slightly. Cover with oiled clingfilm and leave to prove for a further 45 minutes. If your tray isn't large enough to take all of the buns at once, bake them in a couple of batches.

Preheat the oven to 190°C/Fan 170°C/Gas 5. Remove the clingfilm and bake the buns in the centre of the oven for about 20 minutes until risen and golden brown. Serve warm the day they're made – great spread with butter and drizzled with syrup or honey.

DUTCH CHRISTMAS COOKIES
(Janhagels)

Makes about 14

These are like a spicy shortbread, topped with almonds, cinnamon and sugar, and a traditional Christmas treat in Holland. The Dutch name means 'an unruly mob' – the word 'hagel' or hail meaning multitude. The crumbled topping on the cookies is said to resemble hail. Another story we heard about these goodies is that they are given little children arriving in heaven – aahh, bless!

sunflower oil, for greasing
300g plain flour
200g soft light brown sugar
1 tsp fine sea salt
1 tsp ground cinnamon
½ tsp ground mixed spice

200g cold butter, cut into cubes
1 medium egg, beaten

TOPPING
50g rough-cut demerara or white sugar cubes
50g flaked almonds

Preheat the oven to 180°C/Fan 160°C/Gas 4. Grease a 30 x 20cm cake or brownie tin with sunflower oil and line the base with baking parchment.

Mix the flour, sugar, salt, cinnamon and spice in a large bowl. Add the cubes of butter and rub them into the flour with your fingertips until the mixture resembles wet sand.

Stir in the beaten egg with a wooden spoon, then bring the dough together and knead lightly to form a smooth ball. Break the dough into 6 rough pieces and place these in the prepared tin. Press the dough with your hands and then the back of a spoon until the pieces are joined and cover the base of the tin evenly.

Put half the demerara or sugar cubes in a pestle and mortar and pound them into small pieces. Transfer these to a bowl and pound the rest. Toss all the crushed sugar with the flaked almonds, sprinkle the mixture over the dough and press it firmly into the surface with your fingers.

Bake in the centre of the oven for 35–40 minutes until light golden brown and firm. Leave to cool in the tin for 2–3 minutes, then cut into neat fingers. Leave to cool completely or serve just warm.

DUTCH APPLE CAKE
(Appelkoek)

Serves 8–12

We ate this at a lovely bakery in Scheveningen, a seaside resort in the
Netherlands, and very delicious it was. Frank, the baker, didn't want to give
us his recipe, which is a closely guarded secret, so here's our very own version.

225g butter, plus extra for greasing
4 medium eggs
225g golden caster sugar
finely grated zest of ½ lemon
2 tbsp fresh lemon juice
250g plain flour

1 heaped tsp baking powder
1½ tsp ground mixed spice
500g medium cooking apples,
  such as Bramley
25g flaked almonds
1 tsp ground cinnamon

Preheat the oven to 190°C/Fan 170°C/Gas 5. You'll need a 2.25-litre, fairly shallow ovenproof
dish. A lasagne dish is ideal but a round one will work just as well.

Melt the butter in a medium pan over a low heat, then set it aside to cool for a few minutes.
Using an electric hand-whisk, beat the eggs with 150g of the caster sugar for 5 minutes until the
mixture is pale and thick. The whisk should leave a thick trail when lifted from the bowl. Beat
in the lemon zest and juice, then beat in the melted butter until smooth.

Sift the flour, baking powder and spice over the top of the egg mixture, then beat them in using
the whisk's slowest setting. Beat the mixture just enough so that no lumps of flour remain, but
be careful not to over beat or you will lose too much volume from the eggs and sugar.

Grease the dish with butter, then pour in the cake batter and put it to one side while you prepare
the apples.

Peel the apples, cut them into quarters and remove the cores. Cut each quarter in half again
lengthwise and then slice thinly – don't worry if the pieces are a little uneven. Put the apples in
a large bowl and toss them with the almonds, 50g of the remaining sugar and the cinnamon.
Scatter the spiced apples over the cake batter and sprinkle them with the rest of the caster
sugar. Bake in the centre of the oven for 35–40 minutes until well risen and golden brown.
Serve warm or cold with some cream.

DUTCH BUTTER CAKE
(Boterkoek)

Serves 8

This is a favourite cake in the Netherlands – and a favourite of ours now too. It's dense, buttery and tasty and really easy to make. The Dutch love their dairy, and their butter is deservedly famous. Butter plays a starring role in this simple cake.

175g butter, softened, plus extra for greasing
250g caster sugar
1 tsp almond extract
1 large egg

250g plain flour
½ tsp baking powder
1 tsp milk
40g flaked almonds

Preheat the oven to 190°C/Fan 170°C/Gas 5. Grease a 23cm spring-clip cake tin and line the base with baking parchment.

Put the butter, sugar and almond extract in a large bowl and beat with a wooden spoon until pale, light and fluffy. Beat the egg in a separate bowl, then pour all but 1 teaspoon of the beaten egg into the creamed mixture and stir well to combine.

Add the flour and baking powder and mix to a smooth, fairly stiff batter. Spoon the batter into the cake tin and spread evenly. Stir the milk into the reserved beaten egg and brush over the surface of the cake, then sprinkle on the flaked almonds.

Bake the cake for 40 minutes until risen and golden brown. It should look glossy and a little bit sticky when it is cooked, but will sink a little as it cools.

BELGIAN POTATO TART
(Aardappeltaart)

Serves 6–8

A Belgian classic, this is like a well dressed up potato dauphinoise and it goes down a treat with a glass of Belgian beer.

1kg medium potatoes (preferably Maris Piper)
25g butter
1 medium leek, trimmed and sliced
125g thickly sliced smoked ham, cut into 1cm dice
300ml double cream
¼ whole nutmeg, finely grated
flaked sea salt

freshly ground black pepper

PASTRY
250g plain flour, plus extra for dusting
a good pinch of flaked sea salt
125g cold butter, cut into cubes
1 medium egg, whisked with 1 tbsp cold water

Start by making the filling. Bring a saucepan of water to the boil. Peel the potatoes and cut them into slices about 3mm thick. Carefully drop these into the hot water and bring it back to the boil. Cook the potatoes for 3 minutes, then drain them in a colander and rinse them under cold running water until cool. Leave to drain.

Melt the butter in a large non-stick frying pan and fry the leek over a medium heat for 4–5 minutes until softened but not coloured, stirring regularly. Add the ham to the pan, toss lightly with the leek and remove from the heat. Leave to cool. Place a sturdy baking tray in the oven and preheat the oven to 200°C/Fan 180°C/Gas 6.

For the pastry, put the flour in a food processor and add the salt, crumbling it in your fingers as you do so. Drop the cubes of butter on top and blitz on the pulse setting until the mixture resembles fine breadcrumbs. Pour the egg and water on to the flour and butter mixture with the motor running and continue blending until the dough begins to form a ball.

Gather the pastry and turn it out on to a lightly floured surface, then knead it quickly into a ball. Roll it out on a lightly floured surface until it is about 5mm thick and use it to line a 23cm loose-based tart tin. Press the pastry well into the base and sides and trim the edges.

Pour the cream into a jug and season with a good grating of nutmeg, plenty of salt and freshly ground black pepper. This pie can take a lot of seasoning. Arrange a layer of potatoes in the pastry case, top with a scattering of leeks and ham and a slurp of the seasoned cream. Repeat the layers twice more. Slowly pour the remaining cream mixture into the pastry case, stopping every now and then to allow the cream to find its way between the layers.

Bake the pie on the preheated baking tray for 45–55 minutes until pale golden brown and cooked through. Test it is ready by piercing the centre of the pie with a sharp knife. The potatoes should be very soft and the cream firm. Remove from the oven and leave to stand for 10 minutes before lifting from the tin. Serve warm or cold in wedges.

BELGIAN PIZZA
(Flammekueche)

——

Makes 1 large or several small pizzas

This is a pizza for anyone who doesn't like tomatoes and it makes a good simple supper dish. It's great street food too and can be folded in half and eaten as you wander round the market. The Belgian name means 'flame tart', a reference to the time when it was baked in a wood-fired oven.

BASE	TOPPING
300g plain flour, plus extra for dusting	1 tbsp olive oil
2 tsp fine sea salt	200g bacon lardons or rindless smoked
175ml water	streaky bacon rashers, cut into 2cm slices
1 tbsp olive oil	500g onions (3–4 medium onions),
	cut in half and thinly sliced
	200ml crème fraiche

Place the flour in a large bowl and stir in the salt, then make a well in the centre. Mix the water and olive oil together and pour them into the well. Immediately start stirring with a wooden spoon and then your hands to form a soft, spongy dough. Turn this out on to a floured surface and knead for 10 minutes until it's smooth and elastic. Cover with a clean tea towel and leave to rest while you make the topping.

Heat the oil in a large non-stick frying pan and fry the bacon for 3–4 minutes until the fat begins to crisp. Remove with a slotted spoon, leaving as much oil and fat as possible in the pan, and set aside on a small plate. Tip the sliced onions into the pan and cook over a low heat for about 15 minutes until well softened but not browned, stirring occasionally. Remove the onions from the heat and leave to cool slightly for a few minutes. The onions will brown when the flammekeuche is baked.

Preheat the oven to 240°C/Fan 220°C/Gas 9. Line a large baking tray with baking parchment. Roll out the dough on a lightly floured surface into a rough circle or rectangle about 3mm thick – the thickness of a £1 coin. Lift the dough with the rolling pin and transfer it to the prepared tin. You can make several smaller flammekueche if you prefer.

Spread the crème fraiche over the dough, leaving a 2cm border all the way around the edge. Scatter the onions and then the bacon on top. Bake in the centre of the oven for 16–20 minutes or until the base is crisp and lightly browned around the edges and the topping is bubbling. Serve piping hot.

maïs amandel
Kaneel
2.95
Bij aankoop van
Brood
nu Bikers
Bread
Voor € 1.00
alleen vandaag

BAKERY SONNEMANS LUNCH

BELGIAN CHOCOLATE TRUFFLE CHEESECAKE

Serves 10

Oh boy! Chocolate, cheesecake – what's not to like? And everyone knows that Belgian chocolate is the best in the world. Just thinking about this makes us weak at the knees – not one for the faint hearted.

FILLING
200g dark Belgian chocolate, broken into pieces
500g full-fat soft cheese
200ml soured cream
150g caster sugar
3 large eggs

BISCUIT CRUST
sunflower oil, for greasing
300g chocolate oat biscuits, such as Hobnobs
50g butter, melted

DECORATION
Belgian chocolate truffles,
100g white cooking chocolate, for grating, or icing sugar

Lightly oil a 23cm loose-based spring-clip cake tin and line the base with baking parchment. Put the chocolate for the filling in a heatproof bowl and place it over a pan of simmering water. Check that the bottom of the bowl isn't touching the water. When the chocolate has melted, remove it from the heat and stir until smooth, then set aside to cool for a few minutes.

To make the crust, break up the biscuits roughly, then put them in a food processor and blitz them into crumbs. Add the melted butter and blend until mixed. Tip the mixture into the tin and press it firmly and evenly over the base. Pop the tin into the freezer to harden.

Preheat the oven to 180°C/Fan 160°C/Gas 4. Bring a kettle of water to the boil. Put the cheese, soured cream, sugar and eggs in a food processor and blend until smooth. With the motor running, slowly add the melted chocolate and blend until thoroughly combined.

Remove the biscuit base from the freezer. Take 2 large sheets of foil and place them on the work surface, one across the other. Take the cake tin out of the freezer and place it in the centre of the foil and bring the foil up around it to create a bowl shape. Place the whole thing in a roasting tin. Pour the chocolate mixture on to the biscuit base. Then carefully pour hot water from the kettle into the roasting tin until it rises almost halfway up the sides of the cheesecake.

Bake the cheesecake in the centre of the oven for 35–45 minutes. It's ready when the chocolate mixture is almost firm but retains a slight wobble. Turn the oven off, but wedge a folded tea towel in the door and leave the cake to cool in the oven with the door ajar for at least 1 hour. Remove, cover with clingfilm and chill for at least 4 hours or overnight before serving. To serve, loosen the sides of the tin with a knife and release the spring clip. Slide the dessert off the base of the tin on to a plate. Decorate with the chocolate truffles and dust with grated white chocolate or icing sugar. For utter luxury, serve with some cream. Yum, yum!

BELGIAN BRIOCHE
(*Craquelin*)

Makes 12

We think this is a very clever little recipe. These brioche-style buns have a sweet surprise at their centres – a sugar cube soaked in orange liqueur. They're delectable and well worth the effort.

125ml whole milk

2 tbsp caster sugar, plus 1 tsp

1 x 7g sachet of fast-action dried yeast

sunflower oil, for greasing

500g plain flour, plus extra for dusting

1 tsp fine sea salt

finely grated zest of 1 well-scrubbed orange

4 medium eggs, beaten

175g butter, softened

2 tbsp orange liqueur such as Mandarine Napoleon or Cointreau (or freshly squeezed orange juice)

12 white sugar cubes

1 egg yolk, beaten, to glaze

Pour the milk into a small saucepan and stir in the teaspoon of sugar. Place over a low heat for a few seconds until the milk is just warm, then remove from the heat and pour the milk into a bowl. Stir in the yeast and leave to stand for 10 minutes until a froth floats on the surface.

Grease a 12-hole muffin tin or brioche moulds with oil. If using moulds, place them on a baking sheet. Sift the flour into a bowl and stir in the salt, the remaining 2 tablespoons of sugar and the zest. Make a well in the centre and pour in the yeast mixture. Tip the eggs on top and immediately begin stirring with a wooden spoon, bringing all the ingredients together to form a soft, spongy dough. Turn the dough out on to a floured surface and knead gently for about 5 minutes until smooth. Gradually start adding the butter, a teaspoon at a time, kneading constantly until it's all incorporated. This will take about 10 minutes and the dough will be very sticky.

Clean the surface and your hands, then dust the surface with more flour and knead the dough for 10 minutes. Form the dough into a ball and place in a big, well-oiled bowl. Cover loosely with oiled clingfilm and leave in a warm place for 1½ hours or until it has doubled in size.

Pour the liqueur or orange juice on to a saucer and dip the sugar cubes in so they absorb the liquid. Place the dough back on a floured surface and punch it with your knuckles to knock it back. Knead again for 1 minute. Divide the dough into 12 pieces. Roll 1 piece into a ball and, holding it in the palm of 1 hand, press it with your other hand to flatten. Place a soaked sugar lump in the centre and bring up the sides all the way around, pressing the sides together to seal the sugar inside.

Place the sugar-filled ball in the muffin tin or brioche mould, seal-side down. Repeat with the remaining dough and sugar lumps. Glaze the tops with beaten egg yolk, cover with oiled clingfilm and leave in a warm place for a further 45 minutes until well risen. Preheat the oven to 220°C/Fan 200°C/Gas 7. Bake the brioche buns in the centre of the oven for 10 minutes, then reduce the temperature to 180°C/Fan 160°C/Gas 4 and cook for another 10 minutes until they are well risen and golden brown. Remove the buns from the oven, loosen the sides with a round-bladed knife and turn them out on to a wire rack. Leave to cool or serve warm.

RIESLING WINE & MEAT PIE
(Rieslingspaschteit)

***

Makes about 6

This is a traditional Luxembourg dish – a wonderful meat pie into which a fragrant Riesling jelly is poured and left to set. We were very keen to track down this recipe, as when Dave worked in Luxembourg for a couple of years a while back, he used to eat one of these pies for his lunch every day. He was thrilled to meet them again and introduce them to me.

FILLING	3 sheets of leaf gelatine
200g beef mince	freshly ground black pepper
500g pork mince	
2 medium carrots, finely diced	**PASTRY**
1 medium onion, finely diced	200g butter
1 bunch 0f parsley, finely chopped	600g plain flour, plus extra for dusting
1 tsp dried marjoram	1 tsp salt
½ tsp flaked sea salt	1 medium egg
3 tbsp brandy	1 egg yolk
1 medium egg, beaten, to glaze	150ml water
300ml Riesling wine	

For the filling, mix the beef and pork mince with the carrots, onion, parsley, marjoram, salt and freshly ground black pepper. Stir in the brandy, cover and chill for 2–3 hours, or overnight.

To make the pastry, melt the butter over a low heat, then set aside to cool for a few minutes. Put the flour in a large bowl and stir in the salt. Beat the egg and egg yolk with the water in a separate bowl. Stir the eggs and water into the flour, then gradually add the melted butter and form into a ball. Put this in a bowl and leave to rest for 2 hours.

Divide the pastry into 6 portions and roll them out into rectangles measuring about 18 x 20cm. Trim them neatly and keep the trimmings to make pastry chimneys. Divide the mince mixture into 6 sausage shapes and place 1 sausage in the centre of each piece of pastry. Brush the edges lightly with beaten egg.

Fold up the 2 short sides of the pastry and then bring the long sides up and over the filling to enclose and fully seal the meat inside. Turn the parcel over, with the edges underneath, and place it on a baking tray lined with baking parchment. Very lightly score the pastry with the point of a sharp knife – don't go too deep or the pastry will split when it bakes. Repeat with the remaining filling and pastry.

Preheat the oven to 180°C/Fan 160°C/Gas 4. Using the point of a knife, make a small hole in the centre of each parcel and enlarge the hole with the tip of your little finger. Roll out the pastry trimmings and cut into strips about 1.5cm wide. Roll these around your little finger, then place a rolled strip in each hole to make a 'chimney', rising roughly 1cm out of the pastry. Brush generously with beaten egg and bake for 45 minutes. Remove from the oven and leave to cool.

Put the gelatine sheets in a bowl of cold water and leave them for 5 minutes until softened, then squeeze out the excess water over the sink. Meanwhile, heat the wine very gently until just warm enough to melt the gelatine, plop the squeezed gelatine sheets into the warm wine and stir until dissolved. Transfer the mixture to a jug and leave to cool.

Put a small plastic funnel in one of the pastry 'chimneys' and pour the wine into the pie. Take it slowly and let the wine find its way through the pie for a few seconds before adding more. Stop when the wine reaches halfway up the chimney. Repeat with all the pies. Put in the fridge and leave to set for at least 3 hours.

GERMANY

We discovered some spectacular baked goods in Germany – including potato bread – and we baked real proper Black Forest gateau. We even found time to enjoy a few beers and beer snacks. Auf weidersehen, pet!

PORK WRAPPED IN PASTRY
(Schweinelende in Blätterteig)

You've heard of Beef Wellington – this is Pork Wilhelm! In this classic German recipe, pork tenderloin is wrapped in ham and buttery pastry, then baked to juicy perfection. Use a 375g of ready-made puff pastry if you want to save a bit of time.

1 tbsp finely chopped fresh rosemary leaves
1 tsp flaked sea salt, plus extra for sprinkling
½ tsp coarsely ground black pepper, plus extra for sprinkling
1 tbsp sunflower oil
1 pork tenderloin (about 500g), trimmed of fat and sinew
6–7 slices of German air-dried ham, or prosciutto

75g Emmental cheese, finely grated
1 medium egg, beaten, to glaze

PASTRY
175g plain flour, plus extra for dusting
a good pinch of fine sea salt
50g cold lard, cut into cubes
50g cold butter, cut into cubes
2–3 tbsp cold water

Mix together the rosemary, salt and pepper on a plate and roll the pork in the seasoning until lightly coated. Heat the oil in a frying pan and fry the pork over a high heat for 4–5 minutes until lightly browned on all sides, turning every now and then. Remove and leave to cool.

To make the pastry, sift the flour and salt into a bowl. Add the lard and butter and rub them into the flour with your fingertips until the mixture resembles breadcrumbs. Using a round-bladed knife, slowly stir in just enough of the water for the dough to come together. Make the dough into a ball with your fingers, then shape it into a fat sausage. Leave to rest for a few minutes.

Arrange the ham in slightly overlapping slices on a piece of clingfilm. Put the cooled pork on top and wrap it tightly in the ham, using the clingfilm to help cover the pork completely. Preheat the oven 200°C/Fan 180°C/Gas 6.

Place the pastry on a lightly floured surface and roll it out to make a rectangle about 38 x 26cm, or just a little longer than the length of the pork tenderloin. The pastry should be at least 3 times as wide as the pork and about 3–4mm thick. Sprinkle half the cheese over the pastry, leaving a 2cm border around the outside. Place the ham-wrapped pork on top, removing and discarding the clingfilm as you go. Sprinkle the pork with the remaining cheese. Brush the pastry border with beaten egg and bring up the short sides of the pastry to cover the ends of the pork. Bring up the long sides and wrap the pork like a parcel, pressing firmly to seal.

Place the parcel, seam-side down, on a baking sheet lined with baking parchment. Brush with more beaten egg to glaze, then sprinkle with a little extra salt and pepper if you like. Bake the pork parcel for 35–40 minutes until the pastry is golden brown and the pork is tender and cooked through. Remove the pork from the oven and leave it to rest for 10 minutes, covered loosely in foil. Transfer it to a board and cut off the ends where the pastry is thickest. Cut the roll into 4 thick slices and serve hot..

GERMAN POTATO BREAD
(*Kartoffelbrot*)

Makes 1 loaf

This is a deliciously moist, soft bread, which is perfect with white asparagus soup (opposite). It really is a multi-purpose bread and great for sandwiches or fried.

375g potatoes (preferably Maris Piper), peeled and cut into even chunks (300g peeled weight)
1 tsp dried fast-action yeast
1 tsp caster sugar
1 tbsp sunflower oil, plus extra for greasing
1 tsp fine sea salt
300g strong white flour, plus extra for kneading (or 100g strong wholemeal flour and 200g strong white flour)
1 tsp onion seeds

Place the potatoes in a large saucepan – you need exactly 300g to make the bread so check the weight once they are peeled. Cover the potatoes with cold water, bring to the boil, then reduce the heat slightly and cook for 15–20 minutes until they are tender but not falling apart. Drain the potatoes in a colander over a bowl and reserve the cooking liquid. Return the potatoes to the pan and toss over a very low heat for 2-3 minutes until any excess liquid has evaporated.

Pour 75ml of the warm cooking liquid into a large bowl and leave to cool for a few minutes. When it's lukewarm, sprinkle over the yeast. Stir in the sugar and leave in a warm place for about 10 minutes until a light foam appears on the surface. If you're using a mixture of wholemeal and white flour, add an extra tablespoon of the cooking liquor.

Mash the potatoes with the oil in the saucepan until they're as smooth as possible, then stir in the yeast mixture and salt. Mix well with a wooden spoon and gradually add the flour, a few tablespoons at a time, stirring well before adding more. When the dough becomes too stiff to stir in the flour, turn it out on to the work surface and knead the remaining flour into the dough. Don't be tempted to add more water or the dough will become too sticky to work with.

Knead the dough for 10 minutes until soft and pliable. Place it in a lightly oiled bowl, cover loosely with lightly oiled clingfilm and leave to rise in a warm place for 45–60 minutes, or until well risen and spongy to touch.

Knock back the dough with your knuckles and shape it into a rough ball. Flatten the ball on a floured surface until it is about 2cm thick, then bring the sides up to the middle to give a rustic surface to the bread. Pinch lightly to seal and sprinkle on some wholemeal flour for additional texture on the outside of the loaf. Place it on a lightly oiled and floured baking sheet, rough-side up, and leave to prove in a warm place for a further 30 minutes.

Preheat the oven to 220°C/Fan 200°C/Gas 7. Score the dough with a knife along the pinched join and sprinkle the top with the onion seeds. Bake the loaf in the centre of the oven for 35 minutes until well risen and crusty on top. Cool on a wire rack.

GERMAN WHITE ASPARAGUS SOUP
(Spargelsuppe)

Serves 4–6

White asparagus, or spargel, is the most popular variety in Germany and this soup is a must during the spargel season, which begins in mid-May. We visited an asparagus grower, picked some stems and cooked them right away in this lovely delicate soup. It can also be made with green asparagus if you can't find the white kind.

500g white asparagus
50g unsalted butter
1 shallot, finely chopped
700ml chicken stock
70ml crème fraiche

2 egg yolks
1 tbsp dry fino sherry
2 tbsp chopped parsley, to garnish
sea salt flakes
white pepper

First peel each asparagus stalk from the tip to the cut end. Chop off the tips and set them aside, then cut the stalks into 1cm pieces.

Melt the butter in a saucepan and sweat the shallot for about 5 minutes until translucent – don't let it brown. Add the chopped asparagus stalks, keeping the tips aside, and sweat them gently with the shallot for another 5 minutes.

Pour in the stock and simmer until the stalks are very tender. This will take 20–30 minutes, depending on the thickness of the stalks. Tip everything into a food processor and blitz until very smooth, then pour the soup back into the saucepan. Bring the soup back to a simmer and add the reserved asparagus tips. Cook gently for about 5 minutes until the asparagus tips are just cooked through.

Mix the crème fraiche, egg yolks and sherry in a small bowl. With the pan off the heat, stir this mixture into the soup and continue to stir gently for a couple of minutes until the egg yolks have thickened the soup. Warm through over a very gentle heat, stirring constantly and taking care not to break up the asparagus tips.

Serve the soup garnished with a sprinkling of parsley and a generous slab of well-buttered German potato bread on the side. Phwoar!

MEAT & CABBAGE BUNS
(Beirocks)

Makes 20

There are lots of different versions of these fab meat-filled buns. We made some and took them a zoigl – a kind of mini beer festival – where they went down really well.

1 tbsp caster sugar
300ml warm water
1 x 7g sachet of fast-action dried yeast
500g strong white flour, plus extra for dusting
1 tsp fine sea salt
1 tbsp sunflower oil, plus extra for greasing

FILLING
2 tbsp sunflower oil
500g lean minced beef
2 large onions, finely chopped
1 small white cabbage

1 tbsp fine sea salt
½ tbsp ground white pepper
1 tsp coarsely ground black pepper
1 tbsp caraway seeds
1 tsp cumin seeds
1 tsp fennel seeds
1 tsp ground cumin
100ml water
50g butter, melted

TO SERVE
mustard and pickles

Stir the sugar into the warm water in a bowl. Sprinkle over the yeast and stir it lightly, then leave for 10 minutes until a light foam floats on the surface. Mix the flour and salt in a bowl and make a well in the centre. Stir the oil into the yeast mixture and slowly pour it all into the flour, mixing with a wooden spoon and then with your hands to form a soft dough. Knead the dough on a floured surface for about 10 minutes until it's smooth and elastic. Put the dough in a lightly oiled bowl, cover with oiled clingfilm and leave it to rise in a warm place for 30–45 minutes.

To prepare the filling, heat the oil in a large non-stick frying pan over a medium heat and gently fry the beef and onions until lightly browned, stirring regularly. Remove any damaged leaves from the cabbage, cut it into quarters and discard the tough core. Finely shred the leaves. Stir the cabbage leaves, salt, pepper and all the spices into the pan with the meat. Continue to fry and stir for 3 or 4 minutes more. Add the water, cover the pan and cook gently for 5 minutes until the cabbage is very soft. Remove the pan from the heat, stir the mixture well and leave to cool.

Return the dough to the work surface and knock it back with your knuckles. Knead it lightly again, then divide it into 20 equal portions and roll each one into a ball. Roll out the balls on a lightly floured surface into rounds measuring about 12cm, roughly the diameter of a saucer.

You'll need 2 large baking sheets, lined with baking parchment. Place 2 tablespoons of the filling into the middle of a dough round, leaving a small border around the edge. Brush the border with water and bring the sides of the dough over the filling into the centre and pinch them together to seal. Place the filled bun on a baking tray, with the seam underneath. Repeat until you've used all the dough and filling, then leave the buns in a warm place for about 20 minutes until they have doubled in size. Preheat the oven to 180°C/Fan 160°/Gas 4. Bake the beirocks for about 20 minutes until they are well risen and golden brown. Brush them with the melted butter and serve warm with mustard and pickles – and beer, of course!

GERMAN ONION MUFFINS
(Zwiebel muffins)

Makes 6

Scones can be savoury so why not muffins too? These probably originated in Poland, but they're great in any language. They're lovely served warm with lots of butter.

40g butter	½ tsp flaked sea salt
1 medium onion, finely chopped	2 tbsp finely chopped fresh dill
175 plain flour	250ml buttermilk
1 tsp caster sugar	2 medium eggs
1 tsp baking powder	1 tsp poppy seeds
1 tsp bicarbonate of soda	

Melt the butter in a small pan and gently fry the onion for 10 minutes or until softened and lightly browned, stirring regularly. Set aside to cool for a few minutes. Preheat the oven to 200°C/Fan 180°C/Gas 6. Line a 6-hole muffin tin with paper muffin cases or some squares of baking parchment.

Sift the flour into a large mixing bowl and stir in the sugar, baking powder, bicarbonate of soda, salt and chopped dill. Make a well in the centre. Stir the buttermilk into the onion and break the eggs on top, then stir well with a wooden spoon. Pour the mixture on to the flour and stir lightly until only just combined.

Divide the mixture between the muffin cases, sprinkle with poppy seeds and bake in the centre of the oven for 16–20 minutes until the muffins are puffed up and golden brown. Scrumptious served warm but great cold too.

BLACK FOREST GATEAU
(Schwarzwälder Kirschtorte)

Serves 12

Layers of rich chocolate sponge sandwiched with whipped cream and a tangy
combination of morello cherry jam, dried sour cherries and Kirsch make this the
most delicious cake you'll ever taste! The gateau was invented by baker Josef Keller
(1887–1981), and the Café Schaefer in Triberg still make it to Josef's original recipe.
We baked the cake in the Black Forest at sunset and a little of the magic rubbed off
on this recipe; it's a million miles away from the tired old dessert trolley version.

225g butter, softened, plus extra for greasing
225g caster sugar
160g self-raising flour
65g cocoa powder
½ tsp baking powder
4 medium eggs

FILLING AND DECORATION
340g jar of morello cherry jam
2 x 80g packs of sweetened dried sour cherries
2–3 tbsp Kirsch
100ml cherry brandy
   (ideally morello cherry brandy)
500ml double cream
50g dark chocolate, coarsely grated
fresh cherries, to decorate

Preheat the oven to 190°C/Fan 170°C/Gas 5. Grease 2 x 20cm loose-based sandwich tins and
line the bases with baking parchment.

Put the butter, sugar, flour, cocoa powder, baking powder and eggs into a food processor or
electric mixer and blitz or beat until smooth and thick. If you're using a food processor, you may
need to remove the lid and push the mixture down a couple of times.

Divide the batter between the prepared cake tins and spread it out evenly with a rubber spatula.
Bake for 22–25 minutes or until the cakes are nicely risen and just beginning to shrink away
from the sides of the tins. Remove them from the oven and cool for 5 minutes before turning
out on to a wire rack. Take off the lining paper and leave the cakes to cool. When the cakes are
cold, carefully turn each one on to its side and cut in half with a serrated knife. Place the cakes
back on the wire rack or a board, cut sides up.

Put the jam in a saucepan with the sour cherries and Kirsch and place over a low heat. Bring to
a gentle simmer and cook for 6–8 minutes, stirring, until the jam has melted and the cherries
are beginning to swell. Leave to cool for 15 minutes.

Sprinkle the cherry brandy over the chocolate sponges, then spread 3 of them with the sour cherry mixture and leave to cool. Make sure that the sponge without the cherry topping is from the top half of a cake. Whip 300ml of the cream with an electric hand-whisk until soft peaks form.

Transfer 1 of the sponges (with the cherry topping) very carefully to a cake stand or plate – slide the loose base from one of the cake tins under the sponge to help you. Using a couple of pudding spoons, dollop about a third of the whipped cream gently on top of the cherry mixture. There is no need to spread it out, but try to keep the spoonfuls evenly spaced over the cake. Sprinkle with a little of the grated chocolate.

Top with another sponge and repeat the layers twice more. You should end up with 3 layers of sponge, cherries, cream and chocolate. Place the final sponge on top, with its top surface facing upwards.

Whip the remaining 200ml of the cream with an electric hand-whisk until soft peaks form. Using the flat side of a palette knife, spread about 3 tablespoons of the cream over the top of the cake, taking it all the way to the edge. Spoon the remaining cream into a piping bag fitted with a large, plain nozzle and pipe rosettes around the edge of the cake. Tip almost all the remaining grated chocolate into the centre and sprinkle the rest over the rosettes.

Decorate with fresh cherries if you have some. Keep the cake cool or chill until ready to serve. It's best to eat it the same day as it is made – how could you resist? – but if you need to make the cake in advance, chill it in the fridge for up to 24 hours and allow to stand at room temperature for 30 minutes before serving.

Tip: If you can get hold of a jar of morello cherries in syrup, use them instead of the dried cherries. Simply drain off the syrup and add the cherries to the saucepan with the jam. Don't be tempted to use canned cherries as they have very little flavour. If you can't get hold of fresh cherries for the decoration, jarred morello cherries also make a great alternative.

RIESLING WINE CAKE
(Riesling-wein-kuchen)

Serves 10

We ate this cake on our first day in Germany and loved it so much we had to find out how to make it. This is the recipe we've come up with. You can bake it without wine if you like – simply squeeze the lemon and oranges and use these juices instead.

softened butter, for greasing
12 cardamom pods
4 large eggs
150g soft light brown sugar
finely grated zest of 1 medium unwaxed lemon
finely grated zest of 2 well-scrubbed oranges
100ml sunflower oil
150ml Riesling wine
200g ground almonds
1 tsp baking powder

WINE SYRUP (OPTIONAL)
200ml dry Riesling wine
  (if your wine is fairly sweet,
    reduce the amount of sugar for the syrup)
150g caster sugar

TO SERVE
crème fraiche or whipped cream
fresh redcurrants (optional)
icing sugar, for dusting (optional)

Grease a 25cm spring-clip cake tin and line the base with baking parchment. Put the cardamom pods in a pestle and mortar and bash them until the pods split. Tip them out on to a board and remove the seeds, discarding the pods, then put the seeds back in the mortar and grind them to a powder. Set aside.

Preheat the oven to 180°C/Fan 160°C/Gas 4. Beat the eggs and sugar together in a large bowl with an electric hand-whisk until light and creamy. Add the lemon and orange zest and the ground cardamom, beating until combined. Slowly whisk in the oil and then the wine to make a smooth thick batter.

Toss the ground almonds with the baking powder and fold them into the batter, then pour the batter into the prepared tin. Bake the cake for 25–30 minutes or until it's well risen, golden brown and coming away from the sides of the tin. Remove the cake from the oven and put the tin on a metal baking tray, then leave the cake to cool for 15 minutes.

You can eat the cake just as it is, but to make it extra delicious add the wine syrup. To make the syrup, put the wine and sugar in a small saucepan and cook over a low heat, stirring until the sugar dissolves. Increase the heat and simmer for 5 minutes. With the cake still in its tin, pour the hot syrup over the top, a little at a time, waiting for the syrup to soak into the sponge each time before adding any more. If the cake doesn't absorb the syrup readily, make a few holes in the cake with a skewer and try again. Leave to cool in the tin.

Serve the cake in wedges with spoonfuls of crème fraiche or whipped cream and perhaps a few berries to decorate. Sprinkle with sifted icing sugar if you like.

GERMAN BEE STING CAKE
(Bienenstich)

Serves 8–10

We were told that this cake got its name because the baker who first made it was stung by a bee attracted by the sticky honey topping. Well, it's a good story anyway! The original cake didn't contain jam but we love the fruity flavour of our version, matched with a soft, sweet yeast dough and vanilla cream.

1½ tsp fast-action dried yeast
½ tsp caster sugar
4 tbsp warm milk (must not be too hot)
250g plain flour, plus
25–40g extra for kneading
½ tsp fine sea salt
1 tbsp caster sugar
2 medium eggs, beaten
85g butter, softened, plus extra for greasing

TOPPING
5 tbsp clear honey
½ tsp ground cinnamon
20g flaked almonds

FILLING
300ml double cream
1 tsp vanilla extract
3 tbsp caster sugar
4 tbsp raspberry jam

To make the dough, sprinkle the yeast and caster sugar on to the warm milk in a small bowl and whisk together lightly. Leave in a warm place for 10 minutes or until a light foam forms on the surface.

Sift the flour, salt and caster sugar into a large mixing bowl. Make a well in the centre and pour in the yeast mixture and the beaten eggs. Mix with a wooden spoon until it forms a ball. Turn the mixture out on to a floured surface and knead gently for about 5 minutes until smooth.

Gradually add small amounts of the softened butter, a teaspoon at a time, kneading well in between each addition. It will take about 10 minutes to incorporate the butter fully, and the dough will be very sticky. Flour the surface generously as you knead in the butter. Use 1 hand for kneading and 1 hand for flouring to stop things getting too messy.

Place the dough on a clean floured surface and, using clean hands, sprinkle the dough with more flour and continue to knead lightly for a further 10 minutes or until it is very pliable, smooth and slightly shiny but no longer sticky.

Place the dough in a large lightly oiled bowl and cover with oiled clingfilm. Leave the dough in a warm place for 1 to 1½ hours until it is well risen and spongy. It should have roughly doubled in size.

Grease a 25cm spring-clip cake tin and line the base with baking parchment. Turn the dough out of the bowl and into the cake tin, pressing it with your knuckles to knock out the air and squish the dough towards the sides. Leave to prove for a further 30–45 minutes until doubled in size again.

Preheat the oven to 180°C/Fan 160°C/Gas 4. To make the topping, put the honey in a small saucepan with the cinnamon and heat gently until very runny. Brush about three-quarters of the honey over the dough and sprinkle with the almonds. Bake the cake for 25 minutes until risen and golden brown.

Take the cake out of the oven and brush it all over with the remaining honey (you may need to warm it up a little first). Return the cake to the oven for a further 3–4 minutes. Cool the cake in the tin for 10 minutes, then release it on to a wire rack. Peel off the lining paper and leave the cake to cool completely.

To make the filling, put the cream, vanilla extract and sugar in a large bowl and whisk with electric beaters until soft peaks form. Make sure you don't over whisk the cream, as you want it to billow over the cake. Spoon the filling into a piping bag fitted with a large star nozzle.

Put the cake on its side and carefully cut it in half with a serrated knife. Stir the jam to soften and spread over the base of the cake. Pipe the cream in concentric circles on top. Place the remaining half of the cake gently on top of the cream. Serve immediately or cover loosely and chill until required.

Tip: You can also make the dough in a food mixer fitted with a dough hook. Put the dry ingredients into the bowl and add the yeast mixture and beaten eggs. Mix to form a dough, then gradually add the butter, alternating with a little of the extra flour until a soft, sticky dough is made. Continue to mix until the dough becomes smooth and shiny.

KARSTEN'S ROOTS BREAD

Makes 2 loaves

Karsten is a 'slow baker' and bakes his amazing bread in the traditional way, just like his grandad did. He lets his dough rise for up to 48 hours and says that 'only time and skilled hands, along with years of working with dough, result in the perfect bread'. The bread gets its name from its shape – twisted like the roots of a tree.

8g dried yeast (not the fast-acting type)

8g caster sugar

390ml warm water

650g strong white bread flour

8g salt

oil, for greasing

Sprinkle the yeast and sugar over 100ml of the warm water and leave it to activate for 5 minutes. Tip the flour and salt into a large mixing bowl.

Slowly add the remaining 290ml of warm water to the flour, mixing everything together with clean hands. Add the yeast mixture and, using your hands, mix to a soft dough. Turn the dough out on to a floured work surface and knead for at least 10 minutes. The dough should be very supple and elastic.

Lightly oil a large mixing bowl and place the dough in the bowl. Cover with a clean tea towel and leave the dough to rest for 24 hours (or up to 48 hours) in a cool place, until it has doubled or tripled in size.

Turn the dough out on to a lightly floured surface and knock it back. Cut it into 2 pieces and shape each piece into a roll about 20cm long. Holding a roll of dough at each end, twist it a couple of times and place it on a floured baking tray. Repeat with the other piece of dough.

Preheat the oven to 240°C/Fan 220°C/Gas 9. Place a roasting tin on the bottom of the oven and bring a kettle of water to the boil. Put the tray of loaves on the top shelf of the oven and fill the roasting tin with boiling water from the kettle – be careful as the water will splutter. The boiling water creates steam in the oven and helps make the bread crusty.

Bake the loaves for 10 minutes, then carefully remove the roasting tin of water from the oven and turn the temperature down to 220°C/Fan 200°C/Gas 7. Bake the loaves for a further 10 minutes, until they are well risen and golden. Check they are cooked by tapping their bases – they should sound hollow. If not, bake them for another 5 minutes and check again.

Try to leave the bread to cool for at least 20 minutes before eating!

OUR HOMAGE TO
HORST KLINSMAN'S PRETZELS
(Bretzels)

———

Makes 12

Pretzels, with their unique knotted shape, are a German baking classic and are particularly popular in southern Germany. There are lots of different kinds, but the best known are these salt-topped versions, which we ate at a wonderful bakery run by Horst Klinsman. We've come up with a version of his recipe that works at home.

1 x 7g sachet of fast-action dried yeast	200g strong plain flour, plus extra for dusting
2 tsp sugar	2 tsp salt
300ml warm water	25g butter, cut into cubes
350g plain flour	2 tbsp sea salt flakes

Place the yeast and sugar in a bowl and pour over the warm water. Leave to stand for 4 minutes.

Tip the plain flour, strong plain flour and salt into a bowl, add the butter and rub it in with your fingertips until the mixture resembles fine breadcrumbs. Pour the yeast mixture over the flour and, using your hands, mix to form a soft, smooth dough. Turn the dough out on to a lightly floured surface and knead for 5 minutes until smooth. Put the dough back in the bowl, cover it with a damp tea towel and leave in a warm place for 1 hour until the dough has doubled in size and looks soft and pillowy.

Knock back the dough and cut it into 12 pieces weighing about 80g each. Roll each piece into a ball. Then roll each ball into a 60cm rope that's thicker in the middle than at the edges. Twist the rope into a pretzel shape and place on oiled baking sheets. Repeat to make the rest of the pretzels. Chill them for 1 hour until the surface of the dough has dried out.

Make a deep, horizontal cut with a sharp knife through the thickest part of the pretzels and sprinkle with sea salt flakes. Leave them to rest at room temperature for 15 minutes and preheat the oven to 200°C/Fan 180°C/Gas 6. Bake the pretzels for 20-25 minutes until deep golden brown. Remove from the oven and cool on a wire rack.

If you want an lovely glaze on your pretzels, brush them with a mixture of beaten egg and water before baking.

EASTERN EUROPE

We visited three countries in this region – that's a lot of saddle time. We found lots of fab new recipes during our whistle-stop tour, including some baking gems such as nut rolls and bacon scones.

SAUSAGE & POTATO CASSEROLE
(Oravska pochutka)

Serves 6

Sausages and sauerkraut are a marriage made in heaven and this traditional baked dish from the Orava region of northern Slovakia makes a hearty supper. Serve with some good bread for a Slovakian super-meal.

1.5kg good potatoes, peeled and cut into bite-sized chunks
2 tbsp olive oil
3 large onions, peeled and sliced
2 tbsp sugar
6 juniper berries

1 tsp ground cumin
1kg sauerkraut
50g butter, cut into cubes
500g sausage meat (seasoned however you fancy, perhaps with herbs or paprika)
flaked sea salt
freshly ground black pepper

Bring a saucepan of salted water to the boil, add the potatoes and cook them gently until just tender. Drain and set aside.

Heat the oil in a large frying pan and fry the onions until softened, then sprinkle in the sugar and cook until the onions are nicely caramelised. Add the juniper berries and cumin and stir well, then add the sauerkraut and simmer until tender. Add salt and pepper to taste. Preheat the oven to 180°C/Fan 160°/Gas 4.

Spread the potatoes over the base of a large baking dish, then scatter the cubes of butter on top. Break up the sausage meat into small chunks and layer these over the potatoes, then pile the sauerkraut mixture on top.

Place the dish in the oven and bake for about 20 minutes until piping hot and bubbling.

SWEET NUT ROLLS
(Kolaches)

—

Makes 4 large ones

Delectable soft, pillowy rolls, filled with a sweet nutty mixture or fruit, these are
like tea cakes and are great for breakfast or tea. We like eating them while they're still
warm with some jam and clotted cream – like a super-charged scone – or toasted.
Honey is good with these too, or even a bit of cheese.

DOUGH	FILLING
325ml whole milk	200ml whole milk
1 tbsp dried yeast	200g caster sugar
850g plain flour, plus extra for dusting	25g vanilla sugar (see page 114)
100g caster sugar	200g nuts (can be hazelnuts, pecans, walnuts),
100g unsalted butter, softened, plus extra for greasing	crushed in a food processor
1 egg	25g white breadcrumbs
½ tsp fine salt	finely grated zest of 1 lemon
1 egg, beaten, for glazing	1 tbsp rum

First make the starter dough. Pour the milk into a small pan and warm gently until it is about
body temperature. Pour the milk into a bowl, then stir in the yeast and 200g of the flour until
dissolved. Stir in a teaspoon of the sugar to feed the yeast and set the mixture aside to begin its
work. This is the starter.

Cream the butter and the remaining sugar in a bowl until pale and light. Add a little more flour
and then beat in the egg and add the salt. Add the milk and yeast mixture and stir, then fold in
the rest of the flour. If the dough is too dry, add a little more milk; if it's too loose, add a bit more
flour. Tip the dough out on to a floured surface and knead it for about 10 minutes until smooth
and elastic. Cover the bowl with a tea towel and set it aside in a warm place until the dough has
doubled in size.

Meanwhile, make the nut filling. Warm the milk in a saucepan over a low heat, then remove the
pan from the heat and add the sugar and vanilla sugar. Stir until all the sugar has dissolved,
then add the nuts, breadcrumbs, lemon zest and rum. Set the filling aside while you finish
the dough.

Grease a large baking sheet. Take the dough, knock it back with your knuckles and divide it into
4 pieces. Roll out 1 piece on a floured surface to about 5mm thick, then cover it with a quarter
of the nut filling. Roll it up like a roly-poly and place it on the greased baking sheet, seam-side
down. Repeat to make 3 more rolls.

Cover the rolls with a tea towel and leave them to rise for 30 minutes. Preheat the oven to
200°C/Fan 180°C/Gas 6. Brush the rolls with beaten egg and bake them for 30–40 minutes
until cooked through and golden. Serve warm.

BREAD PUDDING
(Zemlovka)

Serves 4

This is a kind of bread and butter pud with an Eve's pudding vibe from the fruit, and we like it made with brioche instead of ordinary bread, or even with kolaches (see page 95). Warm and comforting, it's just right on a cold night.

75g raisins	3 eggs
100ml cold tea	100g soft brown sugar
3 apples or 3 pears or	2 tsp cinnamon
a mixture	1 tsp freshly grated nutmeg
squeeze of lemon juice	1 tsp vanilla extract
400ml whole milk	½ large loaf, can be a bit stale (or brioche)
125g unsalted butter, plus extra for greasing	1 tbsp brown sugar crystals

First put the raisins in a small bowl, add the cold tea and leave them to soak. Peel, core and slice the apples or pears and keep them fresh in a bowl of water with a squeeze of lemon juice. Grease a baking dish and preheat the oven to 180°C/Fan 160°C/Gas 4.

Gently warm the milk in a saucepan, then add the butter and allow it to melt. Set the milk and butter aside to cool to lukewarm.

Put the eggs, sugar, cinnamon, nutmeg and vanilla in a bowl and beat with an electric hand-whisk until well combined. Whisk in the buttery milk.

Tear the bread into pieces, keeping the crusts on or off depending on how posh you are, and layer them in the greased baking dish. Strain the raisins, discarding the tea, and scatter them over the bread, then top with the sliced fruit. Pour in the batter and sprinkle on brown sugar crystals. Bake in the preheated oven for about 30 minutes until the pudding has set and has a golden crust on top. Serve with ice cream or custard or try some soured cream for a change.

SLOVAK CHEESECAKE

Makes 12–15 slices

This is a superb baked cheesecake with a deliciously gingery base. We ate this at the Schtoor Café in Bratislava, where they mix traditional recipes with their own exciting new ideas. They very kindly gave us this recipe.

150g ginger biscuits
75g butter, melted, plus extra for greasing
1kg cream cheese
4 eggs
250g icing sugar

finely grated zest of 2 lemons
1 tsp vanilla extract
1 tbsp custard powder
icing sugar, for dusting
8 tbsp jam, for serving

Preheat the oven to 170°C/Fan 150°C/Gas 3½. Grease a 24cm spring-clip cake tin and line the base with baking parchment.

Crush the ginger biscuits in a food processor, or put them in a plastic bag and bash them with a rolling pin, and mix with the melted butter. Press the biscuit mixture into the base of the tin and cook in the preheated oven for 5 minutes. Remove from the oven and leave to cool.

Put the cream cheese, eggs, icing sugar, lemon zest, vanilla extract and custard powder into a large bowl and beat until well combined. Pour the mixture into the tin and cook for 40–45 minutes, until firm around the edge but slightly wobbly in the centre. Remove it from the oven and leave to cool in the tin, then chill for at least 2 hours until firm.

Remove the cheesecake from the tin and place it on a serving plate. Dredge with icing sugar and serve with spoonfuls of your favourite jam.

SLOVAKIAN FRUIT CRUMBLE

Serves 6

**Another recipe from the Schtoor Café, this is an old favourite with a Slovak twist.
A case of East meets West.**

4 ripe plums
1 large apple
6 stalks of rhubarb
8 tbsp muscovado sugar
½ tsp cinnamon
juice of ½ organic lemon
1 tbsp of dark rum (optional)

CRUMBLE TOPPING
175g plain flour
1 tsp allspice
125g muscovado sugar
1 tsp cinnamon
125g butter, diced, plus extra for greasing

Grease a large ovenproof dish with butter and preheat the oven to 200°C/Fan 180°C/Gas 4.

Stone the plums, core the apple and clean the rhubarb, then chop all the fruit into pieces roughly the same size. Put the fruit in a large mixing bowl, add the sugar, cinnamon, lemon juice and rum, if using, and toss well to coat the fruit. Tip the fruit into the ovenproof dish and set aside for the flavours to infuse while you make the crumble topping.

Put the flour, allspice, sugar and cinnamon in a mixing bowl and stir. Add the butter and rub it into the dry ingredients with your fingertips until the mixture resembles coarse breadcrumbs. Sprinkle the crumble mix over the infused fruit. There should be a nice thick layer of crumble topping!

Put the dish on a baking tray in case the juices bubble over, then bake in the preheated oven for about 30 minutes, or until the fruit is bubbling and the topping is golden brown. If you're making the crumbles in individual dishes, cook them for about 15 minutes. Leave to cool slightly and then serve with vanilla ice cream.

UPSIDE-DOWN PLUM TART

Serves 6-8

Plums are hugely popular in Slovakia and used in all sorts of recipes, including pies, breads and liqueurs. Here they star in a Slovak version of tarte tatin – another from the Schtoor Café.

50g butter
200g light brown muscovado sugar
juice of ½ lemon
1 tbsp ground cinnamon
1 tsp vanilla extract

900g (about 10) large firm plums, cut in half and stones removed
1 x 375g sheet of ready-rolled puff pastry
flour, for dusting work surface

Put the butter in a 28cm ovenproof frying pan or a tarte tatin tin and melt over a medium heat. Stir in the sugar and cook for 2 minutes until dissolved. Add the lemon juice, cinnamon and vanilla extract and cook over a low heat for another minute.

Turn the heat down to low and place the plums in the pan, skin-side down, then cook for 5–8 minutes until softened. Remove the pan from the heat and leave to cool for 5 minutes.

Lay the pastry sheet out on a lightly floured work surface and roll out to a width of 30cm if not already wide enough. Using a dinner plate as a template, cut out a 30cm circle from the pastry. Preheat the oven to 200°C/Fan 180°C/Gas 6.

Carefully lift the pastry over the rolling pin and place it over the plums, tucking it down at the edges of the tin. Prick the pastry lightly with a fork and cook for the tart 25 minutes until the pastry has risen and is golden. Leave to cool in the tin for 5 minutes, before inverting the tart onto a serving plate. Serve warm, with whipped cream or vanilla ice cream.

HUNGARIAN LAYERED CASSEROLE
(Rakott krumpli)

Serves 4–5

A one-pot wonder, this baked savoury dish is a great favourite in Hungary and is economical, filling and, even more important, great to eat. Like many Hungarian recipes, it contains paprika, which has been a characteristic ingredient in the cooking of this country since at least the 17th century. They like it hot in Hungary!

900g potatoes, preferably Maris Piper
4 large eggs, at room temperature
150g smoked streaky bacon, cut into thin strips or lardons
150g kolbász (Hungarian sausage), or chorizo or kabanos, skinned if necessary and thinly sliced

300ml soured cream
1 large egg yolk
2 tsp ground paprika
butter, for greasing
flaked sea salt
freshly ground black pepper

Peel the potatoes and cut them into even slices. Bring a large saucepan of salted water to the boil, add the potato slices and cook for about 5 minutes, then drain and set aside.

Bring a medium pan of water to the boil, then gently add the eggs, and bring back to a simmer. Cook the eggs for 9 minutes, then drain them into a sieve and cool under slowly running cold water for 5 minutes.

Preheat the oven to 180°C/Fan 160°C/Gas 4. Heat a large non-stick frying pan, add the bacon and fry for 2 minutes until lightly browned. Add the sausage and cook for 1 minute more, while stirring. Mix the soured cream with the egg yolk and add the paprika, a good pinch of salt and plenty of ground black pepper. Peel and slice the eggs.

Butter a large, fairly shallow ovenproof dish – a lasagne dish is ideal. Arrange half the potato slices in a single layer in the dish and top with half the eggs, sausage and bacon. Pour over half of the cream mixture, then repeat the layers, finishing with sausage and bacon. Pour all the remaining cream over the top and season with a little more ground black pepper. Bake in the centre of the oven for about 25 minutes until hot and bubbling.

BACON SCONES
(*Pogácsa*)

Makes 12

These savoury scones are often mentioned in Hungarian fables and folk tales as the sustaining food that the young man off to conquer the world takes in his backpack. They're traditionally served with beef goulash soup too. You can use pork crackling instead of bacon but these make a heavier scone and we think this version is better with the soup.

60ml milk	2 tbsp grated Parmesan cheese
1 tsp dried yeast	1 tbsp caraway seeds
250g streaky bacon, chopped	120g unsalted butter
500g plain flour, plus extra for dusting	2 large eggs, beaten
1 tsp baking powder	120ml soured cream
½ tsp salt	beaten egg and a drop of water, to glaze

Gently heat the milk in a pan until it is lukewarm, then pour it into a jug and stir in the yeast. Leave it for 15 minutes or so to get working and froth up. Meanwhile, heat a heavy-based pan and fry the bacon bits until crisp and golden. Remove them from the pan and leave to cool.

Sift the flour into a bowl and mix with the baking powder and salt. Stir in the Parmesan cheese and caraway seeds. Put the butter in a small pan over a gentle heat and allow it to melt until it is just liquid. Take the pan off the heat, stir in the soured cream and add the beaten eggs – make sure the butter isn't too hot or the eggs will scramble. Add the cooled crispy bacon and stir in the yeasty milk.

Pour the buttery egg and bacon mixture into a large bowl, then add the flour and other dry ingredients, a little at a time, until everything is combined. Turn the dough out onto a floured work surface and knead for 5 minutes or so until elastic. You can do this with a mixer and a dough hook if you like. Put the dough in a lightly oiled bowl, cover with oiled clingfilm and leave it in a draught-free place for about an hour and a half until it has doubled in size.

Turn the dough out again and knock it back with your knuckles. Dust the dough with flour and roll it out to about 4 cm thick. Cut out rounds with a pastry cutter and place them on a sheet of silicone baking parchment on a baking tray. Using a sharp knife, cut a criss-cross pattern on the top of each one, then leave to rest for another 30 minutes. Preheat the oven to 200°C/180°C/Gas 6.

Brush the scones with the beaten egg and water to glaze and bake them for 25–30 minutes until golden. Eat them warm, split in half and spread with butter. Perfect with beef goulash soup.

BEEF GOULASH SOUP
(Gulyas leves)

Serves 6–8

This is a main meal soup – a soup for heroes. Yes, we know this is a baking book but you have to cook this to go with the pogacsa, the bacon scones opposite, to make a feast fit for Magyar warlord or lady! Don't be scared by the amount of paprika – it works, we promise you.

1kg stewing steak or venison
2 tbsp plain flour
vegetable oil
2 medium onions, diced
4 medium carrots, diced
2 celery sticks, leaves and all, diced
1 red pepper, seeded and diced
5 garlic cloves, crushed
4 tbsp good sweet Hungarian paprika

2 tbsp caraway seeds, crushed
60g tomato paste
3 bay leaves
2 litres good beef stock
4 potatoes, peeled and chopped into small cubes
flaked sea salt
freshly ground black pepper
soured cream and flat-leaf parsley, to garnish.

Trim the meat and cut it into bite-sized chunks. In a large bowl, mix the flour with a teaspoon each of salt and pepper. Add the beef and toss so that all the chunks are dusted with flour.

Heat a tablespoon of oil in a large frying pan and brown the beef in small batches, setting each batch aside while you brown the next. Take care not to crowd the pan or the beef will steam rather than brown.

Meanwhile, heat a little oil in a large heavy-bottomed pan, add the onions, carrots, celery, red pepper and garlic. Cook gently for about 10 minutes until they start to soften.

Add the beef, paprika, caraway seeds, tomato paste and bay leaves, then pour in the beef stock. Stir well, cover the pan and simmer for at least an hour and a half until the beef is starting to get tender. Add the potatoes and continue to simmer for another 30 minutes. Check the seasoning before serving.

Serve the soup in bowls with a generous swirl of soured cream and a good sprinkling of parsley.

GERBEAUD SLICE
(Zerbó)

Makes 15–20 fingers

Budapest has coffee houses and pastries to rival those in Vienna. One of the best-loved Hungarian pastries, zerbó comes from the famous Gerbeaud Café in Budapest. It's made of sweet doughy pastry layered with a filling of nuts and jam and topped with dark chocolate. A cracking good treat.

FILLING
200g walnut halves
150g caster sugar
300g apricot jam

PASTRY
300g plain flour, sifted, plus extra for dusting
1 heaped tsp fast-action dried yeast
50g caster sugar
¼ tsp fine sea salt

50g butter, cut into cubes, plus extra for greasing
4 tbsp whole milk
4 tbsp soured cream
1 medium egg yolk
sunflower oil, for greasing

ICING
50g dark chocolate, broken into squares
50g caster sugar
4 tbsp water

To make the pastry, mix the flour, yeast, sugar and salt in a large bowl. Add the butter and rub it in with your fingertips until the mixture resembles breadcrumbs. Mix the milk, soured cream and egg yolk together. Make a well in the centre of the flour and stir in the egg mixture, first with a spoon and then with your hands to form a soft dough.

Knead the dough very gently on a lightly floured surface for about 2 minutes until smooth. The dough is very light and might be a bit sticky to work with, so take care and sprinkle with a little extra flour if you like. Divide the dough into 3 equal portions. Lightly butter a 20 x 30cm cake tin – a brownie tin is ideal.

To make the filling, put the walnuts and caster sugar in a food processor and blitz until the mixture resembles fine sand. Warm the jam in a small saucepan, stirring it until softened.

Lightly flour a rolling pin and work surface. Roll out a portion of the pastry until it is slightly larger than the tin. Place the buttered tin on top and cut around it to make a perfect rectangle. Lift the dough over the rolling pin and place it gently in the tin, then spread it gently with half the warmed jam. If the dough moves a little, ease it back into place. Sprinkle with half the walnut and sugar mixture.

Roll out another portion of dough and repeat the process, spreading it with the remaining jam and sprinkling it with the rest of the walnut mixture.

Top the stack with a final layer of the rolled dough, again using the tin as a template. Cover with lightly oiled clingfilm and leave it in a warm place for about an hour. The dough will not have risen very much but will feel light and springy to the touch.

Preheat the oven to 180°C/Fan 160°C/Gas 4. Prick the surface of the dough gently all over with a fork and bake for 25–30 minutes, until risen and golden brown. Remove the tin from the oven and leave to cool for 30 minutes before icing.

To make the icing, melt the chocolate with the sugar and water in a bowl over a pan of simmering water. Bring to a gentle simmer, allowing the chocolate mixture to bubble for just a minute, stirring constantly until smooth and shiny.

Pour the chocolate icing over the top of the cooked dough, tilting the tray to allow the icing to reach the edges. Knock the tin gently a couple of times on the work surface to allow the icing to settle. Leave to cool for at least an hour until the icing is set, but do not put in the fridge. Remove carefully from the tin and cut into fingers to serve.

FRIED FLATBREADS
(Lángos)

Makes 6

These are deep-fried flatbreads, served with a sprinkling of cheese and some soured cream. They're a really popular street snack in Hungary and we first ate them in a car park, where a lady was selling them from a stall. She let us have her recipe.

1 x 7g sachet of fast-acting yeast
1 tsp sugar
200ml warm water
25g butter, melted
380g plain flour, plus extra for dusting
a pinch of salt
vegetable oil, for shallow frying

TOPPING
1 garlic clove, cut in half
300ml soured cream
150g hard cheese (Cheddar is fine), grated

Place the yeast and sugar in a bowl and pour over the warm water. Leave to stand for 4 minutes, then pour in the melted butter.

Tip the flour and salt into a bowl. Pour the yeast mixture over the flour and, using your hands, mix to make a soft dough. Turn the dough out on to a lightly floured surface and knead for 6 minutes until smooth. Return the dough to the bowl, cover with a damp tea towel and leave in a warm place for 1 hour until it has doubled in size.

Knock back the dough and cut it into 6 pieces. Roll each piece out on a lightly floured surface and, using a dinner plate as a guide, cut each piece into 25cm circles, which should be about 5mm thick.

Heat the oil in a deep-sided frying pan and shallow fry a round of dough over a medium heat for 2 minutes. Carefully turn it over and fry for a further 2 minutes until puffed up and golden. Remove from the pan and drain on kitchen paper while you fry the rest.

Rub each flatbread with the cut garlic clove and spoon over the soured cream. Sprinkle over the grated cheese and serve.

AUGUSTA'S PUFF PASTRY SLICES
(Kremesh)

Makes about 8

Budapest is full of amazing little coffee houses and they all sell great cakes. We went to the Auguszt coffee house and bakery where we met Augusta – great-granddaughter of the founder – and heard all about the family business. She told us her recipe for their most popular cake, which is a sort of rich custard tart called kremesh.

1 x 350–375g pack of all-butter puff pastry
500ml milk
1 vanilla pod, split
150g caster sugar
25g home-made vanilla sugar

(made by putting used vanilla pods into a jar of caster sugar and leaving to infuse)
75g egg yolks (about 5 medium eggs)
65g plain flour
75g egg whites (2–3 medium eggs)
65g icing sugar

First make the base. Preheat the oven to 200°C/Fan 180°C/Gas 6. Divide the puff pastry into 3 equal pieces and roll each piece into a rectangle about 5mm thick. Place these on a large baking sheet, lined with baking parchment, then bake in the hot oven until puffed and golden brown. Set aside to cool.

To make the custard, put the milk in a saucepan with the split vanilla pod and bring to the boil, then leave to cool. Mix the 150g caster sugar with the vanilla sugar and egg yolks in a bowl and beat until pale and creamy. Slowly add the flour to form a smooth paste.

Make sure that the milk has cooled a little, or the eggs will scramble when added. Remove the vanilla pod, dry it and put it into your vanilla sugar jar. Slowly add the milk to the egg, sugar and flour and mix together to form a smooth rich custard.

Pour the custard into a saucepan and place it on the heat, then stir continuously until it has thickened. Keep the heat low or the custard will curdle. Set the custard aside.

Whisk the egg whites and icing sugar together until they form stiff peaks. Gently fold the whisked egg whites into the still warm custard until just combined. This mix should be light and stiff!

Now build the kremesh. Lay 2 sheets of baked puff pastry out, then spread each one with a thick layer of custard. Carefully lay 1 custard-topped pastry sheet on top of the other, then top with the third sheet of puff pastry to form a custard club sandwich. Using a very sharp knife, cut the kremesh into portions and serve.

CURLY PIES
(Placinta creata)

Makes 4

These pies are served in Transylvanian cafés and they are a great roadside snack. They're a bit like little pizzas really and you can pick your own filling. Very easy to make and they can be cooked in the oven or on top of the stove.

PASTRY
200ml sparkling mineral water
a pinch of salt
1 tbsp sunflower oil
270g plain flour, enough to form a soft dough

2 eggs, beaten
100ml plain yoghurt

FILLING
ham, chorizo, cheese, mushrooms,
whatever you fancy

Pour the mineral water into a mixing bowl and add the salt and oil. Fold in the flour, adding enough to make a soft dough, then put the dough in the fridge to chill for about 30 minutes. This makes it easier to roll out.

Preheat the oven to 180°C/Fan 160°/Gas 4. Take the dough out of the fridge and divide it into 4 balls. Roll out each ball as thinly as you can, then place a round chopping board or a plate underneath, letting the edges of the pastry overlap. This makes a kind of template for your filling.

Place a thin layer of filling over the pastry spreading it out as far as the edges of the plate or board underneath. Don't overdo the filling – a little goes a long way. Fold the edges of the pastry in towards the middle to form a nice pleated curly pie. Don't worry if it looks a bit rustic – the folds make the curls in your curly pie. Repeat to make the remaining pies in the same way and place them on a baking tray.

Beat the eggs with the yoghurt and brush the mixture over the pies. Bake them for about 40 minutes until they are cooked through and have a lovely golden crust. Serve with a salad.

BISCUIT SALAMI
(Salam de biscuiti)

Makes 1 big salami

This tastes fantastic but it was born out of necessity. At one time in Romania, it was hard to get gas for cooking, so baking was difficult, but this cake just needs a bit of melting and no oven. Eggs could be hard to come by too, but there's no need of them in this sticky treat. It's great to take on a picnic.

50g sultanas or nuts	150g caster sugar
50ml dark rum	75g unsalted butter
500g shortbread biscuits	50g cocoa powder
250ml strong coffee	½ tsp vanilla extract

If using sultanas, put them in a small bowl with the rum and leave to soak for 20 minutes or so.

Break the biscuits up by hand into rough chunks and put them in a large bowl. Add the rum-soaked sultanas, if using, or the nuts and rum.

Bring the coffee to a gentle boil, add the sugar and stir until dissolved. Add the butter and allow it to melt, while stirring, then add the cocoa and mix well. Pour this onto the biscuit mixture in the bowl and stir with a big wooden spoon until everything is well combined.

Take a large sheet of foil and fold it in half. Spoon the mixture down the centre and roll it up to form a salami shape. Leave to cool, then chill in the refrigerator.

When it's set, slice into pieces, just like salami.

TELEVISION CAKE
(Televizor)

Makes at least 9 squares

When telly first came to Romania, programmes started at around 8pm each evening and when you first switched on the set, it was just a mass of lines – like a test card. That's how the television cake got its name – from the side it looks like Romanian telly! Of course, it's also brilliant to eat when you're watching TV, Romanian or not.

BISCUIT LAYERS
50g butter, plus extra for greasing
250g flour, plus extra for dusting
1 tsp cocoa powder
50g caster sugar
50ml milk
1 tsp of baking powder, soaked in 1 tbsp milk
1 egg, beaten

SPONGE
4 eggs, separated
250g caster sugar
2 tbsp water
2 tbsp plain flour

CREAM FILLING
250g caster sugar
3 tbsp flour
400ml milk
200g butter
20ml rum

ICING
2 tbsp sugar
2 tbsp cocoa powder
2 tbsp milk
50g butter

First make the 2 biscuit layers. Grease 2 baking trays, which should be slightly bigger than your cake tin, which should be 30cm square, and dust them with flour.

Sift the flour into a bowl, then stir in the cocoa powder and sugar. Add the butter, rubbing it in with your fingertips, then add the milk, the baking powder and milk mixture and the egg. Mix everything together well.

Preheat the oven to 170°C/Fan 150°C/Gas 3½. Divide the mixture into 2, roll both pieces out and place them on the baking trays. The biscuit layers should be just bigger than the size of the base of the cake tin. Bake for about 15 minutes and then set aside to cool.

Now make the sponge. Turn the oven up to 180°C/Fan 160°C/Gas 4. Grease your 30cm square cake tin and line the base with baking parchment. In a large mixing bowl, beat the egg yolks and sugar until pale, then beat in the water and fold in the flour. Beat the egg whites with an electric hand-whisk until stiff, then gently fold them into the flour mixture with a palette knife or a metal spoon. Use a cutting action to fold the mixture and do your best to keep the air in the

egg whites as there is no raising agent in this cake. Pour the mixture into the cake tin and bake the sponge for about 40 minutes until golden and cooked through. Remove the cake from the tin and leave to cool on a wire rack. Using the cake tin as a template, cut the biscuit layers into squares the same size as the sponge.

To make the cream filling, mix the sugar with the flour in a small saucepan and add the milk. Bring to the boil and cook, stirring constantly, until the mixture thickens. Allow it to cool a little, then add the butter and stir in the rum. Set aside to cool.

Now put the cake together. Place a biscuit layer on a board and top with about half the cream filling to a thickness of about 1cm. Carefully place the sponge cake on top and spread with the rest of the cream. Finish with the remaining biscuit layer.

To make the icing, mix the sugar and cocoa powder in a saucepan, add the milk and butter, then bring to a simmer. When the butter has melted, stir well and remove the pan from the heat. Spread the mixture over the top of the cake and leave it to cool. Cut the cake into square chunks to serve.

ROMANIAN SWEET BREAD
(Cozonac)

Makes 12–15 slices

This is a fab sweet bread that's served all over Romania, especially for celebrations such as Christmas and New Year. The fillings vary from region to region but we liked this one. You can also use poppy seeds, choc chips, sweet curd cheese and sultanas.

DOUGH
20g fresh yeast
200g caster sugar
500g flour, plus extra for dusting
200–250ml warm milk
4 egg yolks
1 egg
a pinch of salt
zest of 1 lemon
½ tsp vanilla extract

3 dsrtsp rum
100g butter, melted
1 egg yolk, mixed with 1 tbsp milk, to glaze

FILLING
150g ground nuts
100g caster sugar
1 dsrtsp cocoa powder
zest of 1 lemon

In a jug, mix the yeast with a spoonful of the sugar and 2 tablespoons of the flour. Pour in the warm milk and set aside for the yeast to activate.

Put the rest of the flour in a large mixing bowl and made a well in the middle. Beat the egg yolks with the whole egg and add them to the flour with the rest of the caster sugar and the salt. Add the lemon zest, vanilla extract and rum and mix well.

When the yeast mixture has doubled in size, add it to the mixing bowl and stir well to bring everything together. Tip the dough out on to a floured surface and knead for about 15 minutes until very elastic. Slowly add the melted butter and knead until all the butter has been incorporated. Cover the bowl with a tea towel and leave it in a warm place until it has doubled in size.

To make the filling, mix all the ingredients together to make a paste.

Put the dough on a floured work surface and roll it into a rectangle, then cover it with a layer of the filling paste. Roll it up like a roly-poly and cover it with a tea towel, then leave it in a warm place to double in size again. This will take 40 to 50 minutes.

Preheat the oven to 190°C/170°C/Gas 5. Place the bread on a baking tray and brush it with the egg yolk and milk mixture. Bake for 30 minutes, then turn the oven down to 160°C/Fan 140°C/Gas 3 and cook for another 15–20 minutes or until golden. Serve in generous slices.

AUSTRIA

Even the French admit that Austria is the birthplace of the finest patisseries, and there is no better place to find them than Vienna. It's the land of Sachertorte and Esterhazy torte – more tortes than you can shake a stick at!

MINCED PORK MEATLOAF WITH SOURED CREAM

(Faschierter rahmbraten)

Serves 4

This very traditional Austrian dish is probably the moistest meatloaf we've ever tasted. It's deeply savoury and really easy to make. We cooked it at a pumpkin farm in Austria, where we found out that pumpkin oil is one of the country's main crops. How about that?

1 tbsp sunflower oil
1 large onion, finely diced
1 garlic clove, crushed
500g minced pork or a mixture of beef and pork mince
175g fresh white breadcrumbs
1 tbsp dried marjoram or 2 tbsp freshly chopped marjoram leaves
1 tsp caraway seeds
1 tsp flaked sea salt
1 tsp coarsely ground black pepper
2 medium eggs, beaten
500ml beef stock (preferably fresh stock)
150ml soured cream
a few sprigs of fresh marjoram, to garnish (optional)

Preheat the oven to 190°C/Fan 170°C/Gas 5. Heat the oil in a large frying pan and gently fry the onion for 5 minutes or until softened, stirring occasionally. Add the garlic and cook for 1 minute more, stirring constantly.

Tip the onion and garlic into a large bowl and add the mince, 150g of the breadcrumbs, the marjoram, caraway seeds, salt and pepper. Mix everything well with clean hands, then add the beaten eggs and mix again. Form the mixture into a rough ball.

Place the ball in the centre of a sturdy roasting tin and shape it into a long loaf, about 4cm high. Sprinkle the reserved breadcrumbs on top and pat them lightly into the outside of the loaf. Pour 300ml of the beef stock around the base of the meatloaf.

Bake in the centre of the oven for 20 minutes, then pour the remaining stock into the tin and return to the oven for 10 minutes until cooked through. Transfer the meatloaf carefully to a warmed serving platter and cover loosely with foil.

Place the roasting tin over a medium heat and simmer for a few minutes until the juices are well reduced – you should have about 100ml of liquid in the tin. Stir in the soured cream and warm through gently, stirring constantly, then season to taste with salt and pepper. Strain the sauce through a sieve into a small jug. Garnish the meatloaf with some fresh marjoram sprigs if you have some and serve with the hot sauce.

Tip: To check the meatloaf is cooked right through, remove it from the oven and insert a metal skewer into the centre. Hold it there for a few seconds, then remove and lightly pinch the end. If the heat has penetrated through the meat and cooked it, the skewer should feel hot. Press the spot where the skewer was inserted and the juices should run clear. If there is any sign of pinkness, return the meatloaf to the oven and cook for a further 10 minutes before testing it again.

HAM SOUFFLÉ
(Schinkenauflauf)

Serves 4–6

Like a lot of the Austrian savoury dishes we tried, this soufflé is quite light and delicate – and exceptionally tasty. Just the thing to get you yodelling in the valleys.

1 tbsp sunflower oil
1 small onion, finely diced
½ red pepper, seeded and finely diced
½ green pepper, seeded and finely diced
50g butter, plus extra for greasing
50g plain flour
300ml whole milk

1 tbsp Dijon mustard
1 tsp flaked sea salt
½ tsp coarsely ground black pepper
100g Emmental cheese, coarsely grated
200g thickly sliced smoked ham, cut into small cubes
4 large eggs, separated

Generously butter the inside of a 2-litre soufflé dish or a similar deep ovenproof dish. Place the dish on a baking tray. Heat the oil in a large non-stick frying pan and gently fry the onion and peppers for 5 minutes until softened but not coloured, stirring occasionally. Set them aside.

Melt the butter in a non-stick saucepan over a low heat and stir in the flour. Cook for 30 seconds, stirring constantly. Gradually add the milk, stirring well in between each addition. Bring to a gentle simmer and cook for 4–5 minutes, stirring constantly until the sauce is smooth and very thick. Season with the mustard, salt and pepper, then remove from the heat. Stir in the cheese, onion, peppers and ham. Beat the egg yolks and stir them into the sauce.

The dish can be prepared ahead to this point. Cover the sauce with clingfilm to prevent a skin forming, cool, then chill for a few hours if necessary. Remove the film and stir the sauce well.

Preheat the oven to 190°C/Fan 170°C/Gas 5. Whisk the egg whites in a large clean bowl until they are stiff but not dry. Using a large metal spoon, stir roughly a fifth of the egg whites into the cheese sauce to loosen it, then tip the sauce into the bowl with the remaining egg whites and fold it in gently, taking care not to lose too much volume.

Spoon or slowly pour the mixture into the prepared dish and bake immediately for 35 minutes or until the soufflé is well risen and golden brown but still slightly soft in the centre. Serve at once before it has a chance to sink.

CHOCOLATE CAKE
(Schokogugelhopf)

Serves 10

You'll need a gugelhopf or ring-shaped cake tin for this Viennese cake, which is served with afternoon coffee in the wonderful cafés of that city. We made it by the side of a mountain road on the Grossglockner, the highest peak in Austria, where it tasted even more amazing.

150g butter, plus 2 tsp, softened
50g ground almonds, plus 1 tbsp for dusting
150g dark chocolate, broken into pieces
150g icing sugar, sifted
4 large eggs, separated
125g self-raising flour
½ tsp baking powder

ICING AND DECORATION
125g dark chocolate
40g butter
1 tbsp golden syrup
15–20g flaked or slivered almonds
sugar crystals (optional)

Grease the cake tin with the 2 teaspoons of butter. Sprinkle the tablespoon of almonds into the tin and shake until the inside of the tin is completely coated with a light dusting of almonds.

Melt the chocolate in a heatproof bowl set over a pan of simmering water. Remove the bowl from the heat and stir the chocolate until smooth, then leave to cool for at least 15 minutes.

Preheat the oven to 190°C/Fan 170°C/Gas 5. Put the butter and icing sugar in a large bowl and cream them together until smooth and light. Add the egg yolks, 1 at a time, beating well between each addition. Beat in the cooled chocolate, then the 50g of almonds, flour and baking powder.

Whisk the egg whites in a large, clean bowl with an electric hand-whisk until they are stiff but not dry. Stir about 2 heaped tablespoons of the egg whites into the chocolate mixture to loosen it, then gently fold in the rest with a metal spoon.

Pour the mixture into the cake tin and bake the cake in the centre of the oven for 35–40 minutes until it is well risen and beginning to shrink away from the sides of the tin. Leave the cake to stand for 2 or 3 minutes, then gently run a knife around the sides and turn it out on to a wire rack to cool.

To make the icing, melt the chocolate with the butter and syrup in a heatproof bowl over a pan of simmering water. Remove from the heat and stir until smooth, then leave to cool for 5 minutes. Slowly drizzle the icing over the cake and allow it to slide slowly down the sides. If the icing moves too quickly or doesn't cover the cake properly, let it cool for a few more minutes and then try again. Work slowly to get the best coverage. Leave the iced cake to stand for 10 minutes, then scatter with the almonds and sugar crystals if using. Set aside for an hour or so until the icing is set before serving.

ESTERHAZY TORTE

This famous cake, popular in Austria and Hungary, was created in honour of Paul III Anton, Prince Esterházy (1786–1866), of the Austro-Hungarian Empire. It is an amazing construction of four layers of sponge cake, sandwiched with butter cream, and it looks sensational. We've included a touch of coffee, which is not traditional, but you can flavour the icing with half a teaspoon of vanilla extract, if you prefer, and add an extra teaspoon or two of water until you reach the right consistency. Note that this cake contains raw egg.

40g butter, plus extra for greasing
100g blanched hazelnuts
8 medium eggs, separated
250g caster sugar
25g plain flour

CHOCOLATE & COFFEE BUTTER ICING
125g butter, softened
250g icing sugar, sifted
1 heaped tbsp cocoa powder
2–3 tsp Camp chicory and coffee essence

WHITE GLACÉ ICING
1 medium egg white
200g icing sugar, sifted

DECORATION
40g flaked almonds
25g dark chocolate, broken into squares

Preheat the oven to 190°C/Fan 170°C/Gas 5. Melt the butter in a small saucepan and set it aside. Grease 2 x 20cm loose-based sandwich tins and line the bases with baking parchment.

Put the hazelnuts on a baking tray and bake for 10 minutes or until they are lightly browned. Halfway through the cooking time, take the baking tray out of the oven and swirl the hazelnuts around. Leave the hazelnuts to cool, then put them in a food processor and blitz until they are as finely ground as possible. Brown the flaked almonds for the decoration in the same way but don't blitz them to a powder. Set them aside for later.

Using an electric whisk, beat the egg yolks and sugar together in a large bowl until very light and fluffy, then beat in the melted butter. Sift the flour over the top, add the hazelnuts and fold in gently until just combined.

Wash the electric whisk and dry it well, then whisk the egg whites in a large bowl until stiff but not dry. You should be able to turn the bowl upside down without them sliding out.

Fold a quarter of the egg whites into the hazelnut mixture to loosen, then gently fold in the rest. Don't mix too much or you will lose the volume.

Spoon half the mixture into the tins and spread it evenly. Bake for 12–14 minutes until risen and light golden brown. The cakes are ready when they are just beginning to spring back from the sides of the tin. Remove them from the oven and loosen the sides with a knife. Turn the cakes out on to wire racks lined with baking parchment, remove the baking parchment from the cakes and leave to cool. Wash the tins, grease and line them once more. Use the rest of the cake batter to make 2 more cakes in exactly the same way and leave them to cool.

To make the butter icing, beat the butter, icing sugar, cocoa and coffee essence in a large bowl until very light and creamy. Place 1 of the cakes, shiny side up, on a flat tray lined with baking parchment and spread it with a third of the butter icing. Top with 2 more cakes, spreading the butter cream in between each layer. Leave the top of the cake naked and ready for the white glacé icing.

Finely chop the toasted almonds and press them into the sides of the cake as evenly as you can. Place the cake in the fridge for at least 1 hour for the butter icing to set, then transfer very carefully to a serving plate or cake stand.

Melt the dark chocolate for the decoration in a small bowl over a pan of simmering water or in the microwave. Stir until smooth, then leave to stand for 10 minutes away from the heat.

To make the glacé icing, whisk the egg white very lightly in a bowl with a large metal whisk. Next, using a wooden spoon, gradually stir in the icing sugar until the mixture is smooth, thick and glossy. Pour the icing into the centre of the cake and spread it with a palette knife until smooth. Spoon the melted dark chocolate into a small plastic food bag and squeeze it to one corner. Snip the corner off with scissors to make a simple piping bag.

Pipe the melted chocolate in concentric circles over the icing. Then take a skewer and drag it through the chocolate and icing from the centre to the outside of the cake as if creating the spokes of a wheel. This will give the top of the cake a spider web effect – have a look at the picture on the next page and you'll see what we mean. Put the cake back in the fridge and leave it to set for 2–3 hours. Cut the cake into slim slices and serve with coffee or tea.

EASY SHORTBREAD SQUARES

Makes 12 squares

This is a cheat's version of linzer torte – the classic Austrian lattice-topped tart. It's perfect if you're not very confident with pastry and you want a really easy treat as there is no rolling involved – just grating. Watch your fingers though! You'll need a 20cm loose-based square cake tin.

225g butter, softened, plus extra for greasing
200g golden caster sugar
1 tsp vanilla extract
2 large egg yolks

275g plain flour
1 tsp baking powder
300g seedless raspberry jam
1 tbsp icing sugar

Using an electric hand-whisk, beat the butter with the sugar and vanilla extract until pale and fluffy. Beat in the egg yolks 1 at a time, then sift the flour and baking powder on top. Beat the dough with a wooden spoon until it is smooth and light, then divide it into 2 equal portions and form them into balls. Wrap the balls of dough in clingfilm and freeze for 2–3 hours or overnight.

Preheat the oven to 170°C/Fan 150°C/Gas 3½. Grease a 20cm square cake tin with butter and line the base with baking parchment. Put the jam in a small saucepan and warm it over a low heat until fairly runny, stirring occasionally.

Remove a ball of dough from the freezer and coarsely grate it on to a board, making sure it doesn't become too compacted. Tip the grated dough from the board into the prepared tin and scatter it evenly with your fingertips. Whatever you do, don't press the dough into the tin – it needs to remain in strands.

Using a dessert spoon, drizzle the jam over the grated shortbread, but do not spread it. Take the other ball of dough out of the freezer and grate it coarsely on to the board. Sprinkle it evenly over the jam, again resisting the temptation to press it down.

Bake the shortbread for 40–50 minutes or until pale golden brown and set, then remove it from the oven and leave to cool in the tin. Loosen the sides of the shortbread with a round-bladed knife and carefully take it out of the tin. Peel off the lining paper if necessary. Dust the shortbread with sifted icing sugar and cut it into squares to serve.

VIENNESE WHIRLS

———

Makes 16–18

Like all northerners, we love these. They're not really from Vienna, but give them a twirl all the same. The biscuits have a very light, short texture and need to be piped on to the baking tray, but they're not difficult to make and they taste fab.

250g very soft butter	**FILLING**
50g icing sugar, plus extra to decorate	100g very soft butter
250g plain flour	200g icing sugar, plus ½ tsp for sifting
50g cornflour	½ tsp pure vanilla extract
½ tsp pure vanilla extract	75g seedless raspberry jam

Preheat the oven to 190°C/Fan 170°C/Gas 5. Line a baking sheet with baking parchment. Put the butter, icing sugar, plain flour, cornflour and vanilla extract in a food processor and blitz until smooth. You may need to remove the lid and push the mixture down a couple of times with a rubber spatula. Alternatively, put everything in a large mixing bowl and beat with an electric hand-whisk until smooth.

Spoon the dough into a piping bag fitted with a large star nozzle. Pipe 16–18 circles or rosettes of dough on to the baking sheet, spacing them well apart. Each should measure about 6cm in diameter – slightly smaller than a digestive biscuit. Bake the biscuits in the centre of the oven for 12–15 minutes or until they are pale golden brown and firm. Transfer them to a wire rack. Then pipe out the remaining dough and bake in the same way. You should have about 32-36 biscuits in all.

To make the filling, put the butter in a bowl and sift the icing sugar on top. Add the vanilla extract and beat with a wooden spoon or an electric hand-whisk until very light and smooth. Put the jam in a separate bowl and stir until smooth.

Spoon a little jam on to the flat side of half of the biscuits and place them jam-side up on the wire rack. Gently spread the butter cream icing on to the remaining biscuits and place on the jam-topped ones to make biscuit sandwiches. Put the biscuits on a serving plate and dust with sifted icing sugar before serving.

Tip: Try sandwiching the biscuits with melted chocolate instead of jam and butter cream icing. Delicious!

SACHERTORTE

Serves 10–12

This very rich chocolate cake was first made in 1832 by Franz Sacher, an apprentice in the kitchens of Prince von Metternich (1773–1859), an Austrian politician and diplomat. The prince had ordered a special dessert to be made for some important guests, but on the day, his head chef was ill and Franz Sacher took on the task – with great success. Years later the cake became the subject of a court case when Demel's, a famous Viennese pastry shop, and the Hotel Sacher, owned by a member of Franz Sacher's family, contested the right to call their cakes the 'genuine' sachertorte. Demel's claimed that they had bought the right to produce the cake from the grandson of the creator. After seven years of wrangling, the matter was settled out of court and the Hotel Sacher won the right to label their cakes 'the original sachertorte'. We were shown how to make 'sachertorte reloaded', an updated version, by the chef at the Café Central in Vienna and very good it was, but we've stuck to the trad recipe here.

200g dark chocolate, broken into pieces
175g icing sugar, sifted
175g very soft butter, plus extra for greasing
6 medium eggs, separated
50g ground almonds
100g plain flour
1–2 tbsp whole milk
250g apricot jam

CHOCOLATE COATING
200g dark chocolate, broken into pieces
65g butter
2 tbsp golden syrup

Melt the chocolate in a heatproof bowl over a pan of gently simmering water. Remove the pan from the heat, take the bowl carefully off the pan (remember it will be hot) and stir the chocolate until smooth. Leave to cool for at least 20 minutes, but do not allow it to set. If the chocolate is too hot it will melt the butter when added to the cake batter.

Preheat the oven to 180°C/Fan 160°C/Gas 4. Grease a 23cm spring-clip cake tin with butter and line the base with baking parchment. Using a large wooden spoon or an electric whisk, beat the icing sugar and butter together in a large bowl until very light and creamy. Beat in the egg yolks 1 at a time.

Add the ground almonds and flour and beat well, then stir in the cooled, melted chocolate. Whisk in enough milk to give the batter a soft, dropping consistency.

Using clean beaters and a very large bowl, whisk the egg whites until they are stiff but not dry. Stir about a quarter of the egg whites into the chocolate mixture to loosen it, then tip everything into the bowl with the remaining egg whites and fold in very gently. This may take longer than you think, but keep working gently but thoroughly until all the egg whites are incorporated.

Spoon the cake batter into the prepared cake tin and bake the cake in the centre of the oven for 40–45 minutes, until it is well risen and firm to the touch. The cake should just have started shrinking away from the sides of the tin when it is ready. Remove from the oven and leave to cool in the tin. The cake will sink, but this is normal.

Gently remove the cake from the tin and peel off the baking parchment. Very carefully cut it in half through the middle with a serrated knife – a long bread knife is perfect. Try to keep the pieces as even in thickness as possible. Place the cakes cut sides up on a wire rack above a small tray.

Put the jam in a saucepan and heat gently until softened, stirring constantly, then press it through a fine sieve. Spoon 2 tablespoons of the sieved jam on to 1 of the cakes and spread it out evenly, then sandwich with the other cake. Turn the cake over so that the flat base is facing upwards on the rack and gently brush it all over with the remaining jam. Heat the jam for a few seconds if it has cooled too much to brush.

To make the chocolate coating, melt the chocolate with the butter and golden syrup in a heatproof bowl over a pan of gently simmering water. Remove from the heat, take the bowl carefully off the pan, then stir the mixture until smooth. Leave to cool for 15 minutes.

Pour all of the chocolate mixture on to the centre of the cake and allow to slowly dribble down the sides. Bounce the wire rack gently on the work surface to encourage the icing to flow evenly and give a smooth surface to the cake. Leave the coating to cool and set for at least 5 hours. Do not put the cake in the fridge – the coating will become dull if it gets too cold.

Decorate with a ribbon if you like. You can even pipe the word 'sacher' in melted chocolate with a plain nozzle if you like, just before the chocolate coating is set.

LINZER TORTE

Serves 8–10

This is often said to be the oldest cake in the world and dates back to at least 1653, but no one knows who invented it. There are lots of variations and the oldest known recipe is in a cookbook that was written 350 years ago. Named after the Austrian city of Linz, which is justly proud of this delicious creation, the linzer torte has a crumbly pastry base, a jam filling and a lattice top. This is our version – it's a sort of posh jam tart really.

150g caster sugar

150g plain flour, plus extra for dusting

150g ground almonds

a good pinch of ground cinnamon

150g cold butter, cut into cubes

1 medium egg, beaten

200g good quality raspberry jam

½ tsp icing sugar, to decorate (optional)

Put the sugar, flour, almonds and cinnamon in a large mixing bowl and stir until well combined. Add the cubes of butter and rub them into the flour mixture with your fingertips until the mixture resembles coarse breadcrumbs. It should feel quite moist.

Add the egg and stir with a wooden spoon until the dough comes together, then knead lightly into a ball. Weigh the dough and take a quarter away to use for the lattice topping. Roll the rest out into a ball and turn it out on to a well-floured surface.

Flatten the ball with your hands or a floured rolling pin until it is about 2.5cm thick. Place the dough in the centre of a 24cm loose-based, fluted tart tin and press it with your fingers over the base until it is about halfway up the sides of the tin and the tin is evenly covered.

Spread the jam over the dough as evenly as possible. Shape the reserved dough into a fat sausage and roll it out on a well-floured surface to make a rectangle 3mm thick – about the thickness of a £1 coin. Cut the dough into 1.5cm strips. Place the strips over the jam, first in one direction and then the other to create a criss-cross pattern over the filling. Press the edges to seal, pinch off the excess pastry and smooth the joins down with your fingertips. Chill the tart in the fridge for 30–60 minutes.

Preheat the oven to 190°C/Fan 170°C/Gas 5. Put the tart on a baking sheet and bake in the centre of the oven for about 30 minutes or until the almond pastry is pale golden brown. Cool in the tin for 5–10 minutes, then slide it on to a serving platter or board. Decorate with a light dusting of icing sugar if you like and cut it into wedges to serve.

MONICA'S BREAKFAST BREAD
(Godkipferl)

Makes 6

We visited a monastery where Monica, the cook, showed us how to make these crescent-shaped brioche-style breakfast breads – a sort of ancestor of the croissant. She bakes them on Sundays as a special treat for the monks and this is her recipe.

1kg strong white plain flour, plus extra for dusting	15g caster sugar, plus extra for dredging
1 tsp salt	125ml vegetable oil
2 x 7g sachets of fast-action dried yeast	2 large eggs
500ml milk (lukewarm)	1 egg yolk, beaten

Tip the flour into a mixing bowl with the salt and yeast. Pour the lukewarm milk into a separate bowl and mix with the sugar and oil, then beat in the 2 large eggs.

Pour the milk mixture over the flour mix to form a soft dough with your hands. Turn the dough out on to a lightly floured surface and knead for 5 minutes until smooth. Return the dough to the bowl, cover with a clean tea towel and leave to stand for 15 minutes. Dust 2 non-stick baking sheets with flour.

Knock back the dough and divide it into 6 pieces. Take a piece of dough and cut it into 3. Roll or stretch each of the 3 pieces into sausage shapes about 20–25cm long. Pinch the 3 together at one end, then plait the strands and pinch together at the other end. Repeat with the remaining 5 pieces of dough.

Shape each plait into a crescent shape, place them on the floured baking sheets and leave to rest for 5 minutes. Preheat the oven to 180°C/Fan 160°C/Gas 4.

Brush the crescents with the beaten egg yolk and dredge them with caster sugar, then bake for 25 minutes until they are well risen and golden. Take them out of the oven and check that the crescents are cooked by tapping the base; it should sound hollow. Leave to cool on a wire rack.

GEORGE'S FANTASTIC GINGERBREAD
(Lebkuchenteig)

—

Makes enough for 40 biscuits or one gingerbread house

We visited an amazing bakery in the little village of Seckau in Austria and found that their speciality is gingerbread. We met George, who explained to us that his father had developed a recipe to improve on the standard version of gingerbread, which he thought was too dry and brittle. George cooked his family recipe for us and very good it is.

850g honey
100g double cream, whipped
70g butter
350g rye flour
350g plain flour
15g bicarbonate of soda (about 2 tsp)
22g ground ginger
11g cinnamon (about 3 tsp)

150g hazelnuts or almonds (or a mix of both), finely chopped
50g candied peel
50g lemon peel (or more nuts if you prefer)
2 large or 3 medium egg yolks
flaked almonds and glacé cherries, for decoration (optional)
extra beaten egg, for glazing

The dough needs to be made a day before you plan to bake the gingerbread so you do need to think ahead!

Put the honey, whipped cream and butter into a saucepan and gently bring to the boil. Stir in the rye flour and remove from the heat. In a separate bowl, mix the plain flour with bicarbonate of soda and the spices, then add the nuts, peel and eggs and stir everything together well. Add the honey mixture to the flour and spices and knead to make a smooth ball of dough. Cover the bowl with clingfilm and leave it to rest in a cool place for 24 hours.

Next day, preheat the oven to 200°C/Fan 180°C/Gas 6 and line a large baking sheet with greaseproof paper. Roll out the dough into a slab 3cm thick, then, using your favourite cutter, cut out as many shapes as you can fit. Re-roll any leftovers and cut out more shapes. Place the biscuits on the baking sheet and brush with the beaten egg, then decorate each piece with almonds and cherries if you like.

Bake the gingerbread in the preheated oven for 8–12 minutes. Keep a close eye on it though, as gingerbread burns easily. When cooked, the biscuits should have risen and be nut brown and firm to the touch.

Leave them to cool before serving. If you like, you can decorate the biscuits further with a sugar syrup glaze or even dip them in melted chocolate.

GRANDMA BONKA'S APPLE STRUDEL
(Oma Bonka's apfelstrudel)

Makes 24

In Upper Austria, we stayed in a guesthouse run by a lovely lady called Grandma Bonka who, legend has it, makes the best apple strudel in the area. We love her recipe but we have to confess we cheat a bit and use filo pastry instead of her special home-made strudel pastry.

1kg eating apples
50g breadcrumbs
75g caster sugar
50g raisins

1 tsp cinnamon
6 sheets of filo pastry
75g butter, melted

Preheat the oven to 180°C/Fan 160°C/Gas 4. Peel, core and slice the apples and put them in a bowl, then squeeze some lemon juice over them to stop them going brown. Mix in the sugar, raisins and cinnamon and set aside. Spread the breadcrumbs on a baking sheet, put them in the oven and toast until golden brown. Watch the breadcrumbs carefully, as they burn easily.

Place a sheet of filo pastry on a sheet of greaseproof paper and brush the pastry with melted butter. Lay another sheet of filo pastry on top of the first and brush with butter. Continue until you have 6 sheets of buttered filo, stacked on top of each other.

Sprinkle the breadcrumbs over the top sheet of filo pastry, then spoon the apple mixture over the breadcrumbs. Starting from the shorter end of the filo sheet, roll the strudel up like a Swiss roll, using the greaseproof paper to help you. Place the strudel on a non-stick baking tray and brush it with the remaining butter.

Bake the strudel for 35–40 minutes until it is golden brown and the apples are soft. Serve with cream, ice cream or even custard!

ITALY

It's only 150 years since the nation of Italy was born. Until then it was split into many regions and the food still reflects that. Our mission was to get to the country's culinary heart and savour this Mediterranean soul food – way beyond pasta and pizza. And we baked Italy a birthday cake!

EASY FOCACCIA

Makes 1 loaf

This flatbread dates back to Ancient Rome and was originally cooked in the ashes of the fire – 'focus' means hearth or fire in Latin! Before baking, the dough is sprinkled with a topping, such as coarse salt and herbs, and you make little dimples in the surface with your finger. We cooked this by the side of a canal in Venice – very romantic!

500g strong white flour, plus extra for dusting
1 x 7g sachet of fast-action dried yeast
1 tsp caster sugar
1 tsp fine sea salt
2 tbsp olive oil, plus extra for greasing
300ml warm water

TOPPING
3 tbsp olive oil
2 tbsp flaked sea salt
1 tsp coarsely ground black pepper
1 tbsp roughly chopped fresh rosemary leaves
10 tiny sprigs of rosemary

Put the flour, yeast, sugar and salt in a large bowl. Mix the olive oil with the warm water and pour it on to the flour mixture. Stir with a wooden spoon and then bring the mixture together with your hands to form a rough ball.

Turn the dough out on to a lightly floured surface and knead for 5 minutes to make a smooth, pliable and fairly soft dough. Transfer the dough to a lightly oiled bowl, cover loosely with oiled clingfilm and leave to rise for about an hour in a warm place until it has doubled in size.

Lightly oil a large baking tray measuring about 36 x 25cm. Turn the dough out on to a floured surface and knock it back with your knuckles. Press the dough into a rough rectangle, about the size of the baking tray, then carefully place it on the baking tray and ease it out towards the edges. Don't worry too much about how it looks – it's meant to be rustic.

Cover loosely with oiled clingfilm and leave in a warm place for a further 30 minutes to prove. Preheat the oven to 220°C/Fan 200°C/Gas 7. After 30 minutes, the focaccia should look puffed up and spongy. Use your index finger to poke dimples all over the dough right through to the bottom of the tray.

To make the topping, drizzle the focaccia with the 3 tablespoons of olive oil, allowing it to seep into the dimply holes. Sprinkle with the sea salt, black pepper and chopped rosemary. Finish by poking the twiggy sprigs of rosemary randomly into the dough. Bake in the centre of the oven for about 15–20 minutes or until risen and deep golden brown. Serve warm.

Tip: You can vary the toppings for this focaccia, or even add flavourings to the basic dough. Chopped sundried tomatoes, dried chilli flakes and basil oil are all good additions.

PROSCIUTTO, MOZZARELLA & BASIL STROMBOLI

Serves 6

This is a really fantastic recipe for a kind of filled bread, a bit like a rolled-up pizza! It can also be made with ready-made pizza or bread dough and bought tomato pizza sauce. We cooked this at Si's sister's family feast at her house near Florence.

500g strong white flour, plus extra flour for dusting
1 x 7g sachet of fast-action dried yeast
2 tsp flaked sea salt
2 tbsp olive oil, plus extra for greasing
325ml warm water

FILLING
2 tbsp olive oil
1 small onion, finely chopped
2 garlic cloves, crushed
400g can of chopped tomatoes
½ tsp dried oregano
1 tsp caster sugar
8 slices of prosciutto
125g mozzarella
a large handful of fresh basil leaves
flaked sea salt
freshly ground black pepper
good olive oil and balsamic vinegar, to serve

Sift the flour into a large bowl and stir in the yeast and sea salt. Mix the olive oil with the water and stir into the flour. Mix with a large wooden spoon until the dough comes together and forms a soft, spongy ball.

Transfer the dough to a lightly floured surface and knead it for 5 minutes until smooth. Place the dough in a bowl, cover with lightly oiled clingfilm and leave it for about an hour in a warm place or until it has doubled in size.

While the dough is rising, make the tomato sauce. Heat 1 tablespoon of the olive oil in a non-stick frying pan and fry the onion over a low heat for 5 minutes until softened and lightly browned. Stir regularly and add the garlic for the last minute of the cooking time. Tip the tomatoes into the pan and add the oregano and caster sugar. Season with salt and pepper. Place over a fairly high heat and cook the sauce for 5–8 minutes until very thick, stirring constantly. Remove the pan from the heat and leave the sauce to cool.

Roll out the dough on a lightly floured surface into a rectangle measuring about 44 x 32cm. Spread the tomato mixture over the dough, leaving a 2cm border around the edge. Arrange the prosciutto over the sauce. Tear the mozzarella into small pieces and dot over the prosciutto, then scatter the basil leaves on top.

Tuck in the 2 short ends and roll the stromboli up firmly to enclose the filling. Place it, seal-side down, on a large baking sheet lined with baking parchment and leave to rise for 30 minutes. Preheat the oven to 200°C/Fan 180°C/Gas 6. Brush the remaining oil over the dough, season with a little more salt and pepper and bake the stromboli for 25–30 minutes until well risen and golden brown. Slice thickly and serve with some good olive oil and balsamic vinegar to dip it into, and a green salad.

COURGETTE TART
(*Scarpaccia*)

Makes about 12 squares

This recipe is from the Tuscany region of Italy and it's a kind of large savoury pancake, topped with courgettes and other goodies. It makes a lovely little appetiser to serve with drinks. Si's sister told us that it's called 'bad shoe tart'. Apparently, a bad shoe is one that lots of people have worn, so a bad shoe tart is one that you can put anything you like into.

400g small courgettes, with flowers still attached if possible, or 3 medium courgettes
1 tsp fine sea salt
2 medium eggs
75g plain flour
125ml semi-skimmed milk
(or half full-fat milk, half water)

3 spring onions, trimmed and thinly sliced
1 garlic clove, crushed
50g thinly sliced Parma ham, cut into 2cm strips
50g Parmesan cheese, finely grated
3 tbsp virgin olive oil, plus extra for greasing
flaked sea salt
freshly ground black pepper

Trim the flowers from the courgettes and put them to one side. Cut the courgettes into long thin slices – each about the thickness of a £1 coin. Place them in a colander, sprinkling the fine sea salt between the layers, and leave to stand for 20 minutes.

Preheat the oven to 220°C/Fan 200°C/Gas 7. Line a 23 x 33cm Swiss roll tin or similar with baking parchment and brush it with olive oil.

Beat the eggs in a large bowl with the flour and milk (or milk and water), then stir with a wooden spoon to make a smooth batter – like a pancake batter.

Slice the courgette flowers into thin strips, if using. Rinse the courgettes to remove the salt, then pat them dry with kitchen roll or a clean tea towel. Stir the courgettes, courgette flowers, spring onions, garlic, ham and all but 3 tablespoons of the Parmesan cheese into the batter. Season with a pinch of salt and plenty of freshly ground black pepper.

Pour everything into the prepared tin – the mixture shouldn't be more than 1cm thick. Drizzle the olive oil over the top, sprinkle with a little more salt and pepper and bake for 25 minutes or until golden brown and crisp. When the tart is cooked, sprinkle the remaining cheese on top and cut into squares to serve.

DOUGH RINGS
(Tarallini / Taralli)

—

Makes about 35

These dough rings, made in southern Italy, are part-cooked in boiling water before being baked which gives them their characteristic shiny surface. Small ones are called tarallini and the slightly larger ones taralli and the story goes that fishermen would put them on a string around their neck to snack on while at sea. Dunk them in oil and balsamic.

450g strong bread flour, plus extra for dusting
1 tbsp caster sugar
2 tbsp flaked sea salt
175ml white wine
150ml virgin or extra virgin olive oil, plus extra for greasing

FLAVOURING
Use 1 or 2 of these to add extra flavour:
2-3 dried chilli flakes (depending on how hot you want your tarallini)
1 tbsp dried oregano
½ tbsp coarsely ground black pepper
1 tbsp lightly toasted fennel seeds

Put the flour, sugar, salt and flavouring ingredients into a bowl and make a well in the centre. Measure the wine and oil into a jug, then gradually add them to the flour, mixing with a wooden spoon and then with your hands to form a dough. Turn the dough out on to a cool flat surface , such as marble or granite, and knead for 5 minutes. The dough will start out quite dry and stiff but should become more smooth and pliable as you knead. Put the dough in a plastic bag and leave it to rest for 1 hour.

Another way of doing this is to put the dry ingredients in a food processor and add the liquids with the motor running. Mix to a smooth, elastic, pliable dough, then leave to rest as above.

Weigh the dough – you should have about 700g. Take 20g of dough and roll it between the palms of your hands into a smooth, thin sausage measuring about 1cm in diameter and 15cm long. Dab one end with a little cold water and cover with the other end to make a dough ring. Press firmly to seal and put it on a lightly oiled tray. Make more rings in the same way until all the dough is used up.

Bring a large saucepan of lightly salted water to the boil. Preheat the oven to 190°C/Fan 170°C/ Gas 5. Drop 8–10 dough rings into the boiling water and return to the boil. Cook until the rings rise to the surface of the bubbling water, then remove with a slotted spoon and drain on a wire rack. Cook the rest of the rings in the same way.

Brush a large baking tray with oil. Place the part-cooked rings in rows on the tray. You can put them fairly close together as they won't rise or spread. Bake in the centre of the oven for 30 minutes until pale golden brown. Remove from the oven and leave to cool before serving.

PISTACHIO TUILES
(Tegole ai pistacchi)

Makes 16–18

These thin crispy biscuits are thought to look like traditional roof tiles – 'tegole' means tile in Italian, like 'tuile' in French – but they look more like Pringles to us. They are great way of using pistachios and pine nuts, which grow in many parts of Italy.

25g shelled pistachio nuts
15g pine nuts (the long Italian ones)
50g butter
75g caster sugar

75g plain flour
2 medium egg whites
½ tsp vanilla extract

Preheat the oven to 180°C/Fan 160°C/Gas 4. Line a large baking sheet with baking parchment. Roughly chop the nuts together on a board.

Put the butter, sugar, flour, egg whites and vanilla in a food processor and blend until pale and smooth. You may need to remove the lid and push the mixture down once or twice with a spatula.

Put 6 level tablespoons of the mixture on the baking sheet, spacing them well apart, and spread them with a palette knife to make thin oval shapes. Sprinkle the nuts generously over the top.

Bake the biscuits for about 18 minutes until pale and set in the middle and golden brown around the edges. Take them out of the oven and, working quickly, take each biscuit and place it on a rolling pin, so that the sides overhang and curl around the pin. Leave to cool, then transfer to a wire rack and leave until cold and crisp.

Make 2 more batches of biscuits in exactly the same way. They keep for up to 3 days in an airtight tin.

GRANDMA'S CAKE
(Torta della nonna)

—

Serves 8

Every family has their own version of this traditional Tuscan dessert. It's a kind of custard tart, topped with tasty pine nuts, and it tastes great. We'd go round to Grandma's more often if she made cakes like this.

PASTRY
250g plain flour, plus extra for dusting
50g caster sugar
a pinch of fine sea salt
125g cold butter, cut into cubes
1 medium egg, beaten

FILLING
300ml whole milk

300ml double cream
finely grated zest of 1 medium orange
4 large egg yolks
75g caster sugar
25g plain flour
1 tsp pure vanilla extract
50g pine nuts
1 tsp icing sugar, to decorate (optional)

To make the pastry, sift the flour into a large bowl and add the sugar and salt. Rub the cubes of butter into the flour with your fingertips until the mixture resembles fine breadcrumbs. Make a well in the centre and add the egg. Using a round-bladed knife or your hand, stir the egg into flour mixture, bringing it all together. Knead very lightly and form into a ball.

Turn the pastry out on to a lightly floured surface and roll out until it is large enough to line a 20cm loose-based, fluted tart tin. Trim the edges and prick the base very lightly with a fork. Chill in the fridge for 30 minutes. Save any trimmings for patching the tart case once cooked.

Preheat the oven to 200°C/Fan 180°C/Gas 6. Place the tart tin on a baking tray. Roughly scrunch up a piece of baking parchment slightly larger than the tart tin, unfold it and place it inside the pastry case. Half fill the pastry case with baking beans or dried beans.

Bake the pastry case on the baking tray in the centre of the oven for 20 minutes. Take it out, remove the parchment and beans and put it back in the oven for 5–10 minutes until dry and pale golden brown on the inside. If the pastry has any cracks after the parchment is removed, use the pastry trimmings to patch the pastry before returning it to the oven. Leave to cool for 20 minutes. Reduce the oven temperature to 160°C/Fan 140°/Gas 3.

To make the filling, put the milk and cream in a large saucepan and bring it slowly to a simmer, stirring constantly. Remove from the heat and stir in the zest. Beat the eggs yolks and the sugar together in a heatproof bowl until pale, then stir in the flour and vanilla. Gradually pour the warm milk on to the egg mixture, stirring until thoroughly combined, then return to the saucepan.

Cook the custard over a low heat for 6–10 minutes until it thickens, stirring constantly, but do not allow it to overheat. The custard should coat the back of a spoon when cooked to the right consistency. Leave to cool for 10 minutes.

Put the pine nuts in a dry frying pan over a medium heat and toast them until browned on all sides, stirring regularly. Tip them into a heatproof bowl and leave to cool.

Pour the custard very gently into the pastry case and sprinkle with the pine nuts. Bake in the centre of the oven for about 30 minutes until the custard is set but retains a slight wobble. Leave to cool then cover and chill in the fridge for several hours until set.

Remove carefully from the tin and transfer to a board or serving platter. Decorate by dredging with sifted icing sugar before serving if you like.

ARETINO CAKE
(Il gattó Aretino)

Serves 8

This is a sort of boozy Swiss roll which comes from the city of Arezzo in Tuscany. Aretino means 'from Arezzo'. Different liqueurs can be used but we like Frangelico or Amaretto.

40g butter, plus extra for greasing
5 medium eggs, separated
200g caster sugar
finely grated zest of 1 unwaxed lemon
75g plain flour
75ml Frangelico or Amaretto liqueur

CHOCOLATE CREAM FILLING
150ml full-fat milk
1 medium egg

1 medium egg yolk
75g caster sugar
finely grated zest of ½ small orange
25g plain flour
100g dark chocolate, roughly chopped
a small knob of butter
1 tbsp dark rum
1 tsp icing sugar mixed
   with 1 tsp cocoa powder, to decorate
   (optional)

To make the chocolate cream, pour the milk into a saucepan and bring to a gentle simmer. Pour it into a heatproof jug and set aside. Beat the egg, egg yolk, sugar, zest and flour in a non-stick saucepan with a wooden spoon, then slowly pour in the hot milk, stirring constantly. Place the pan over a low heat and cook for 5–6 minutes or until the sauce is very thick – it should look similar to a stiff béchamel sauce. Stir constantly so that it doesn't become lumpy as it cooks. Remove the sauce from the heat and stir in the chopped chocolate. Stir until the chocolate melts, then stir in the butter and rum. Pour the sauce into a mixing bowl and cover the bowl with clingfilm to prevent a skin forming on the sauce. Leave it to cool and thicken.

Preheat the oven to 190°C/Fan 170°C/Gas 5. Melt the butter for the cake in a small saucepan and set aside. Grease a 23 x 33cm Swiss roll tin and line the base with baking parchment. Using an electric whisk, beat the egg yolks and sugar in a large bowl until very light and fluffy. Beat in the melted butter and lemon zest, then sift the flour on top and beat in until smooth.

Wash the beaters and dry them well. Whisk the egg whites in a large bowl until stiff but not dry. Fold a quarter of the egg whites into the lemon mixture to loosen, then gently fold in the rest. Don't mix too much or you will lose the volume. Turn the mixture into the prepared tin.

Bake the cake for about 15 minutes or until it has risen and is pale golden brown. The sponge should just have started to spring back from the edge of the tin. Remove from the oven and let the cake cool for 2–3 minutes, then turn it out on to a clean, damp tea towel, peel off the lining paper and leave for a further 10 minutes.

While the cake is only just warm, drizzle the liqueur over it and let it soak into the sponge. Spread with the chocolate cream, making sure it is nice and thick. Roll the cake up from one short end, using the tea towel to help keep the shape, and put it on a serving plate. Dust with sifted icing sugar and cocoa powder, if using, to decorate and serve in slices.

CHOCOLATE & HAZELNUT CAKE
(Torta gianduia)

Serves 10

We made this as a birthday cake for Italy, which celebrated the 150th anniversary of its unification in 2011. Gianduia is a specialty of the Piedmont region and it's a mixture of ground hazelnuts and chocolate, now mostly seen as the popular spread called Nutella.

250g whole blanched hazelnuts
200g butter, cubed, plus extra for greasing
200g dark chocolate, broken into squares
6 medium eggs, separated
200g caster sugar, preferably golden

3 tbsp Frangelico hazelnut liqueur
or Amaretto liqueur (or fresh orange juice)

TOPPING
150g Nutella chocolate and hazelnut spread

Preheat the oven to 200°C/Fan 180°C/Gas 6. Put the hazelnuts on a baking tray and roast them in the centre of the oven for 10 minutes, giving the pan a shake every 5 minutes, until they are golden brown. Watch them carefully so that they don't burn. Remove and leave them to cool for a few minutes. Reduce the oven temperature to 180°C/Fan 160°C/Gas 4.

Butter a 23cm spring-clip cake tin and line the base with baking parchment. Place 200g of the hazelnuts in a food processor and blend them until they are fairly finely ground. If you blend the nuts to the consistency of fine breadcrumbs, they should work a treat, but leave a few coarser pieces to add texture. Set the remaining nuts aside.

Put the butter and chocolate in a heatproof bowl and set it above a pan of gently simmering water. Stir occasionally and as soon as nearly all the chocolate has melted, remove the bowl from the pan and continue to let the chocolate melt in the residual heat. Stir in the ground hazelnuts and leave the mixture to cool for 5 minutes.

Beat the egg yolks and sugar together with an electric hand-whisk for at least 5 minutes until pale and creamy, then stir into the chocolate mixture until thoroughly combined. Wash and dry the beaters well. In a clean bowl, whisk the egg whites until stiff peaks form – they are ready when you can turn the bowl upside down without the eggs sliding out. Do not over whisk.

Working quickly, stir the Frangelico, Amaretto or orange juice into the chocolate mixture to soften. Add a couple of tablespoonfuls of the whisked egg whites and stir until thoroughly combined, then gently fold in the remaining egg whites. Spoon the mixture into the prepared tin and bake in the centre of the oven for 35–40 minutes or until the cake is well risen and firm.

Remove the cake from the oven and leave it to cool in the tin for 30 minutes. Undo the spring-clip and invert the cake on to a serving plate, then peel off the lining paper and leave it to cool completely. When the cake is cold, spread it with the Nutella and sprinkle with the hazelnuts that you set aside – these can be whole or chopped, whatever you prefer.

AMARETTO CHEESECAKE

Serves 8–10

This light and lemony cheesecake packs a hefty dose of Amaretto, an Italian almond liqueur, and a dusting of amaretti – little biscuits made from almonds (see page 179).

15g softened butter, for greasing
40g crunchy amaretti biscuits, plus extra for the top
750g ricotta cheese
150g caster sugar

6 medium eggs
100ml double cream
finely grated zest of 1 lemon
4 tbsp Amaretto liqueur

Preheat the oven to 180°C/Fan 160°C/ Gas 4. Grease the base and sides of a 24cm spring-clip cake tin with butter. Put the base of the tin in upside down so that it will be easier to remove the cheesecake once it is ready.

Put the amaretti biscuits in a food processor and blitz them to fine crumbs. If you don't have a food processor, put the biscuits into a strong plastic bag and crush them with a rolling pin instead. Sprinkle the biscuit crumbs over the bottom and the sides of the cake tin, tilting and shaking the tin to get an even coating.

Drain the ricotta cheese and put it in a mixing bowl with the sugar, then whisk with an electric hand-whisk until well combined. Gradually add the eggs, 1 at a time, whisking well in between each addition. Stir in the cream, zest and liqueur. The mixture will be very soft and light.

Pour the mixture slowly into the prepared tin, starting in the middle to avoid disturbing the crumbs. Put the tin on a baking tray and bake in the centre of the oven for 10 minutes. Reduce the oven temperature to 160°C/Fan 140°C/Gas 3 and cook for a further 60 minutes or until the cheesecake is just set. Do not allow it to get too brown. If the cheesecake does start to brown while it is still very wobbly, cover it loosely with foil.

When the cheesecake is ready, turn the oven off and open the door slightly. Wedge a folded tea towel or wooden spoon in the door to keep it ajar and leave the cheesecake to cool completely. This will take 3–4 hours and should prevent the top from cracking. When the cake is completely cool, put it in the fridge and chill for at least 2 hours before removing it from the tin.

Slide a knife around the cheesecake, taking care to retain as much of the crumb base as possible, and gently release it from the tin. Carefully slide it on to a serving plate and crumble over the extra amaretti biscuits. Great served with poached peaches and cream.

AMARETTI BISCUITS

Makes 24

This is our home-made version of the almond biscuits you see in delis and cafés all over Italy. There are loads of variations, some crispy and crunchy, some with soft centres, and we love 'em all. Eat these with a cup of espresso coffee or dunk them into a glass of Marsala wine or Vin Santo.

2 large egg whites
200g caster sugar

½ tsp almond extract
300g ground almonds

Preheat the oven to 190°C/Fan 170°C/Gas 5. Line 2 large baking trays with baking parchment.

Using an electric hand-whisk, whisk the egg whites in a large bowl until foamy. Gradually whisk in the caster sugar, a tablespoon at a time. Whisk in the almond extract, then fold in the ground almonds with a large metal spoon. The mixture will be very stiff but should remain workable.

Spoon the almond mixture into a piping bag fitted with a large plain nozzle. Pipe blobs of the almond mixture on to the trays, spacing them evenly apart. Wet your finger and smooth the top of each biscuit but don't flatten them too much.

Bake 1 tray at a time for 16–18 minutes until the biscuits are crisp and lightly browned. Cool them on the tray for 5 minutes, then transfer to a wire rack. Store in an airtight tin.

Tip: Sprinkle the amaretti with tiny pieces of crushed sugar cube before baking to give them an attractive appearance.

POLENTA BREAD
(Pane di polenta)

Makes 2 loaves

Polenta is made from dried, ground maize (corn) and is used in Italy to make a
thick porridge-like dish that's served with stews and other savouries, or baked and
cut into slices. Polenta can also be mixed with flour to make this great bread –
Italy's take on corn bread.

1 tsp caster sugar
350ml warm water
1 x 7g sachet of fast-action dried yeast
250g plain flour, plus extra for dusting

150g fine polenta (quick cook),
plus extra for dusting
1 tsp fine sea salt
1 tbsp olive oil, plus extra for drizzling

Whisk the sugar and warm water together in a medium bowl, then stir in the yeast very lightly.
Leave aside in a warm place for about 10 minutes or until you can see a beige foam floating on
the surface of the mixture.

Mix the flour, polenta and salt in a large bowl and make a well in the centre. Pour the foamy
liquid and olive oil on to the flour and, using a wooden spoon, slowly mix everything together.
The dough will be quite wet at first but will become firmer as the polenta begins to swell.

As soon as the dough is firm enough to handle, gather it together with your hands and knead
for a couple of minutes. Transfer the dough to a lightly floured surface and knead for 10 minutes
until it is smooth and elastic. Put the dough in a lightly oiled bowl, cover the bowl with a piece
of lightly oiled clingfilm and leave it to rise in a warm place for about an hour or until it has
doubled in size. Line 2 baking trays with baking parchment.

Put the dough back on a work surface lightly dusted with flour and knock it back with your
knuckles. Cut the dough in half with a large knife. Flatten each piece with the palms of your
hands, then bring the sides into the middle and pinch them together. Turn the loaves over and
place them on the baking trays. Cut a cross in the centre of each loaf with the tip of a knife.
Leave to prove in a warm place for a further 45 minutes or until well risen.

Preheat the oven to 200°C/Fan 180°C/Gas 6. Dust the loaves with a little more flour and bake
them, 1 above the other, for 25–30 minutes or until the bread is pale golden brown and the base
sounds hollow when tapped. Cool on a wire rack. If 1 loaf doesn't brown as well as the other, pop
it back in the oven for a few more minutes.

Serve in thick slices with Italian cheese, fresh tomatoes and basil leaves. Drizzle with a little
extra olive oil to serve, if you like.

LIMONCELLO BABAS

Makes 8–12

We love rum babas and this is our Italian version. This is not an authentic recipe, but it's really good and we know you're going to love it. Limoncello comes from southern Italy and is beautifully fragrant liqueur made with lemon peel.

75g sultanas
5 tbsp Limoncello
2 tbsp cold water
225g plain flour
1 x 7g sachet of fast-action dried yeast
½ tsp fine sea salt
4 large free-range eggs
4 tbsp milk
1 tbsp clear honey

115g butter, well softened but not melted
50g chopped mixed peel

SYRUP
400g caster sugar
400ml cold water
finely grated zest and juice of 1 lemon
6 tbsp Limoncello
3 tbsp clear honey

Put the sultanas in a saucepan with the 5 tablespoons of Limoncello and the cold water. Place the pan over a medium heat and bring to the boil, then remove from the heat and leave to cool. Generously butter a 12-hole muffin tin or 8–10 metal rum baba moulds set on a baking tray.

Sift the flour into a large bowl and stir in the yeast and salt. Beat the eggs with the milk and honey. Beat the egg mixture and butter into the dry ingredients with a wooden spoon for about 5 minutes or until very smooth and glossy. Drain the sultanas, reserving the liqueur, and stir them into the batter with the mixed peel.

Spoon the mixture into the tin or moulds and leave in a warm place to rise for about an hour or until roughly doubled the size. Preheat the oven to 190°C/Fan 170°C/Gas 5. Bake the babas for 12–15 minutes or until they are well risen and golden brown.

While the babas are baking, make the syrup. Put the sugar in a saucepan with the cold water and the lemon zest and juice. Heat gently, stirring occasionally, until the sugar dissolves. Bring to a simmer and add the reserved liqueur, the additional 6 tablespoons of Limoncello and the honey. Bubble for a few seconds then remove from the heat. Leave to stand.

Remove the babas from the oven and let them cool in the tin for 5 minutes. Loosen the sides with a blunt-ended knife and turn them out into large, shallow ceramic dish. You may need to put them on their sides, but that's fine. Taste the syrup – take care as it will be hot – and add a little more Limoncello if you like. Pour half the syrup slowly over the babas and leave them for 5 minutes while the liqueur soaks in.

Carefully turn the babas over in the dish. Pour over the remaining syrup and leave the babas for another 10 minutes. Turn once more, then cover and chill in the fridge for at least 2 hours before serving. These babas will keep for 2–3 days in the fridge. Serve with any leftover syrup and lots of double cream.

FRANCE

Ooh la la! We're off to the South of France for biking, baking and sunshine. Could life get any better? We tasted some of the most indulgent baking in Europe, including perfect baguettes, tarts and macaroons, and boy, how we loved them!

PROVENÇAL BREAD
(Pain de Provence)

Makes 1 large loaf

This is a wonderfully fragrant bread, guaranteed to bring the sunshine of Provence to the greyest winter day. It's made with a starter dough, which gets the bread going and helps make it light and airy, but you'll need to start preparations the day before baking.

STARTER DOUGH
5g fresh yeast or 1 tsp fast-action dried yeast plus
1 tsp caster sugar
100g strong white flour
100g rye flour, plus extra for dusting
200ml warm water

BREAD
10g fresh yeast or 2 tsp fast-action dried yeast
1 tbsp fine sea salt
500g strong white flour, plus extra for dusting
325ml lukewarm water
sunflower oil, for greasing
3 tbsp finely chopped fresh thyme leaves
1 tbsp finely chopped fresh rosemary leaves
1 tbsp fennel seeds, lightly toasted

To make the starter dough with fresh yeast, rub the yeast into the flours in a mixing bowl, then add the water and mix with a wooden spoon to form a thick paste. Cover with clingfilm and put the bowl in the fridge for 24 hours. If using dried yeast, sprinkle over the water and stir in the sugar. Leave in a warm place for 10 minutes or until a light foam forms on the surface. Add to the flours and mix to form a stiff paste. Chill in the fridge for 24 hours.

To make the bread, rub the fresh or dried yeast and salt into the flour and set aside. In a large mixing bowl, gently mix half of the prepared starter dough and the 325ml of warm water until sloppy. You can freeze the remaining starter dough for up to 1 month and thaw it overnight in the fridge before using.

Add the just mixed flour, salt and yeast to the large mixing bowl. Using a wooden spoon at first and then your hands, bring both mixtures together to form a ball. Knead on a floured surface for about 10 minutes, then put the dough in a lightly oiled bowl, cover with oiled clingfilm and leave to rise in a warm place for 1 hour.

Carefully ease the dough out of the bowl, put it on a floured surface and gently knock it back with your knuckles. Knead the herbs and fennel seeds into the dough for a few minutes until evenly dispersed, then form into a ball. Place this on a surface lightly dusted with rye flour, flatten it into a large round, then bring in the sides to meet in the middle and pinch hard. Turn the dough over to make a perfect round loaf shape and flatten slightly. Place the loaf on a baking sheet, cover loosely with oiled clingfilm and leave to rise for a further hour. Score the surface lightly with a knife – creating a pattern like the spokes of a wheel

Preheat the oven to 220°C/Fan 200°C/Gas 7. Bake the loaf for 25–30 minutes until well risen and golden brown. The loaf should sound hollow when the base is tapped. Cool on a wire rack.

BRIOCHE SAUSAGE ROLL
(Saucisson brioche)

Serves 8

**This is the Rolls Royce of sausage rolls, made with a large French saucisson
and a rich brioche dough. It's usually baked as one large loaf, but individual rolls
can be made with smaller sausages. You could also use a roll of sausage meat.**

1 large saucisson, or other
soft French sausage

BRIOCHE
1 x 7g sachet of fast-action dried yeast
1 tsp caster sugar
125ml warm milk

500g plain flour, plus extra for dusting
1 tsp fine sea salt
2 tbsp caster sugar
4 medium eggs, beaten
175g butter, softened,
plus extra for greasing
1 egg yolk, beaten, for glaze

To make the dough, sprinkle the yeast and caster sugar on to the warm milk in a small bowl.
Whisk them together lightly, then leave in a warm place for 10 minutes or until a light foam
forms on the surface.

Sift the flour, salt and caster sugar into a large mixing bowl. Make a well in the centre and pour
in the yeast mixture and the beaten eggs. Mix together with a wooden spoon until the mixture
forms a ball.

Turn the dough out on to a floured surface and knead it gently for about 5 minutes until smooth.
Gradually add the softened butter, a teaspoon at a time, kneading well between each addition.
It will take about 10 minutes to incorporate the butter and the dough will be very sticky.

On a clean floured surface and using clean hands, sprinkle the dough with flour and continue
to knead lightly for 10 minutes until the dough is very pliable, smooth and no longer sticky.
Place it in a large buttered bowl and cover with a clean cloth. Leave in a warm place for 1½
hours until well risen and spongy.

Turn the dough back on to a lightly floured surface and knock it back with your knuckles.
Knead for a minute or so, then flatten the dough slightly and wrap it around the saucisson,
pressing the edges firmly to seal. Place it in a lightly buttered 900ml loaf tin and cover loosely
with clingfilm. Leave in a warm place to prove for 45 minutes or until the dough is well risen.

Preheat the oven to 180°C/Fan 160°C/Gas 4. Brush the brioche lightly but generously with
beaten egg yolk and bake for 35–40 minutes until risen and golden brown. Cool it in the tin for
10 minutes, then turn out and cool on a wire rack. Serve in thick slices.

LEMON TART WITH BERRIES
(Tarte au citron)

This is one fresh little French fancy. Mouth-puckeringly citrusy, lemon tart is a French classic, seen in the best patisseries all over the country. If you don't want to make your own pastry, you can use a block of ready-made sweet shortcrust.

PASTRY	FILLING
250g plain flour, plus extra for dusting	6 medium eggs
175g cold unsalted butter, cut into small pieces	225g caster sugar
25g icing sugar	finely grated zest of 2 lemons
1 medium egg, beaten	175ml fresh lemon juice (about 4 lemons)
	250ml single cream
	mixed fresh berries and sifted icing sugar, to decorate

Place a 23cm loose-based fluted flan tin on a baking tray. To make the pastry, put the flour, butter and icing sugar in a food processor and pulse until the mixture resembles fine breadcrumbs. With the motor running, gradually add the beaten egg and blend until the mixture forms a ball. Put the pastry on a sheet of baking parchment dusted with sifted icing sugar and roll it into a circle about the thickness of a £1 coin. Turn the paper every couple of rolls to help create an even shape and rub the rolling pin with flour so that it doesn't stick.

Lift the pastry over the rolling pin and lower it gently into the flan tin. Push the pastry into the base and sides of the tin and leave the excess pastry overhanging the edge. Patch any splits in the pastry to ensure the flan case is completely watertight. Cut off a small amount of the overhanging pastry, wrap it in clingfilm and keep it for patching the cooked tart if necessary. Prick the base lightly with a fork and chill for 30 minutes.

Preheat the oven to 200°C/Fan 180°C/Gas 6. Line the pastry case with crumpled baking parchment and fill with baking beans. Bake the pastry for 25 minutes, then take it out of the oven and remove the paper and beans. Return it to the oven for a further 4–5 minutes until the surface of the pastry is dry and lightly browned. Reduce the oven temperature to 150°C/Fan 130°C/Gas 2. Trim off the excess pastry with a sharp knife, making sure to work slowly so that the pastry doesn't crack. If the pastry has any holes, patch them with the reserved pastry.

To make the filling, put the eggs in a jug and whisk until smooth. Add the sugar, lemon zest and lemon juice and stir with a wooden spoon until well combined. Don't use a whisk or you'll end up with a bubbly tart. Pour the cream into the lemon mixture, stirring well. Return the tart on its baking tray to the oven and pull the shelf out about halfway so that you can fill the tart to the top without moving it and sloshing the contents about. Pour the lemon mixture slowly into the tart case and return it to the oven. Bake for 30–35 minutes or until the filling is just set. It should still wobble a little in the middle. Cool completely in the tin. Remove the tart from the tin just before serving and slide it on to a serving plate or cake stand. Arrange the berries in the middle of the tart and dust with sifted icing sugar to serve.

APRICOT TARTE TATIN

Serves 6

This is an upside-down fruit tart, first cooked by the Tatin sisters at their restaurant in central France. The story goes that it was created by accident but was such a success with the guests that it became a much-loved classic. The apple version is the best known, but apricots work really well too – sunshine on a plate.

75g caster sugar
40g unsalted butter, cubed
300g fresh apricots, halved and stoned
(about 7 or 8 apricots)

375g sheet of ready-rolled puff pastry
plain flour, for dusting
crème fraiche or ice cream, for serving

For caramelising the apricots, you need a small ovenproof frying pan with a base that measures about 20cm in diameter. Put the sugar in the pan and set it over a medium heat. Cook until the sugar first melts and then caramelises and turns golden brown. Don't stir the sugar but swirl it around the pan every now and then.

Remove the caramel from the heat and stir in the butter with a wooden spoon. The caramel will be extremely hot so watch out for splashes and don't dream of tasting it.

Continue stirring for 2–3 minutes as the caramel cools and thickens. It will look oily and separated to begin with, but will become smooth and toffee-like as you continue stirring. When the caramel is smooth, carefully arrange the apricots on top, cut-side down. Leave to cool for 20 minutes.

Unroll the puff pastry sheet on a lightly floured surface and use a rolling pin to roll it out until it is 2cm wider. Place a dinner plate or 25cm cake tin on the pastry and cut around it. Gently slide the pastry on top of the apricots and push down the sides with a round-bladed knife. Prick the surface and chill until 30 minutes before serving.

Preheat the oven to 200°C/Fan 180°C/Gas 6. Bake the tarte tatin for 25 minutes until the pastry is golden and the apricots are cooked. Remove the pan from the oven using an oven cloth to hold the handle of the pan – don't forget it will be very hot.

Leave the tart to stand for a couple of minutes to allow it to settle, then loosen the edges and place a large serving plate or board on top of the frying pan. Very carefully turn it over, using a folded dry tea towel to help you hold it, and allow the tarte tatin to drop gently on to the serving plate. Serve warm with crème fraiche or ice cream.

HAZELNUT & CHOCOLATE VACHERIN

Serves 8

A vacherin is a classy French dessert made of meringue and cream and we think this version is one of the most impressive dishes we've ever created.

HAZELNUT MERINGUE
150g blanched hazelnuts
sunflower oil, for greasing
5 large egg whites
275g caster sugar
½ tsp pure vanilla extract
2 tsp cornflour

FILLING
100g dark chocolate (at least 70% cocoa solids), broken into pieces
500ml double cream
1 tbsp icing sugar, sifted
200ml crème fraiche
400g raspberries
icing sugar, sifted, to decorate

Toast the hazelnuts in a dry frying pan for 4–5 minutes until golden, leave them to cool, then chop roughly. Cut out 3 large rectangles of baking parchment. With a dark pencil and using a plate as a template, draw a 25cm circle in the centre of 2 pieces and a 20cm circle on the third. Lightly grease 2 baking sheets and place the pieces of parchment with the 25cm circles on them, pencil-side down. You should be able to see the circles through the paper.

Preheat the oven to 150°C/Fan 130°C/Gas 2. Whisk the egg whites in a large bowl until stiff but not dry. Gradually whisk in the sugar, a tablespoon at a time, whisking for a few seconds in between each addition. Finally whisk in the vanilla extract and the cornflour until well combined. Fold all but a few of the hazelnuts into the meringue. Set the rest aside for later.

Place large spoonfuls of the meringue on the 25cm circles. Spread the meringue to the edges with a rubber spatula to make 2 large, flattish meringue discs, using a little more than two-thirds of the meringue. Spread the rest of the meringue over the 20cm circle and put it on a third lightly greased baking tray if you have one. Turn the oven down to 120°C/Fan 100°C/Gas ½. Bake the 2 larger meringues, 1 above the other, for 1½ hours, switching between the shelves after 45 minutes, until very lightly coloured. Reduce the oven temperature further if they begin to get too brown. Remove from the oven and leave to cool. Cook the third meringue as above.

Melt the chocolate in a small bowl over a pan of hot water. Stir until smooth, then leave to cool for a few minutes. Whip the cream with the icing sugar until soft peaks form. Stir the crème fraiche to soften it slightly and fold it into the cream.

Put a large meringue disc on a serving plate and spoon over half the cream. Drizzle with a little chocolate and scatter a third of raspberries on top. Drizzle with a little of the melted chocolate. Top with the second large meringue disc and repeat the layers, then top with the smaller meringue. Finish the vacherin by scattering with the remaining raspberries, drizzling with chocolate and sprinkling the reserved nuts on top. Dust with sifted icing sugar to serve.

PAIN AU CHOCOLAT

Makes 14

Seen in every bakery in France, these are made with the same dough as croissants but with a lovely chocolate filling. What a great breakfast! Now, we know you can buy them but home-made are a thing apart so, one weekend, set aside some time and give yourself a real treat. The process does take a while but it's not difficult so give it a go and make your own pain choc to dunk in your breakfast coffee.

BASIC DOUGH
1 tsp caster sugar
225ml warm water
1 x 7g sachet of fast-action dried yeast
450g strong white flour,
plus extra for dusting
25g butter
1 medium egg

FILLING
225g butter, softened
200g dark chocolate, chopped into small
pieces

GLAZE
1 medium egg
1 tbsp caster sugar

In a medium bowl, whisk together the sugar and warm water. Stir in the yeast very gently. Leave aside in a warm place for about 10 minutes or until you can see a beige foam floating on the surface. Cut the butter for the filling into rough 1.5cm cubes and divide it between 3 side plates, then leave to soften at room temperature.

Put the flour and the 25g butter into a large bowl and rub the butter into the flour as if you are making pastry. Make a well in the centre, then whisk the egg into the yeast mixture and pour it all on to the flour. Stir with a wooden spoon and then your hands until the mixture comes together to form a soft, spongy dough. Knead in the bowl for a minute then turn out on to a well-floured surface and knead for 10 minutes until the dough is very smooth and elastic.

Roll the dough out in one direction into a rectangle about 50 x 20cm, sprinkling with extra flour if it begins to stick. Keep the short side facing you. Take a third of the softened butter for the filling and dot it evenly over the top two-thirds of the pastry rectangle, leaving the bottom third empty. Make sure you leave a 2cm border around the butter at the sides, so that it doesn't ooze out when folded.

Bring up the bottom third of dough over the buttered middle of the dough and fold down the top third of the dough to meet the bottom edge. Half seal the edges by pressing with a rolling pin. Turn the dough a quarter turn anti-clockwise, so that the bottom part is now facing right.

Give the dough a little press down with the rolling pin along its length and then roll once again into a rectangle measuring about 50 x 20cm. Repeat the same process using the second plate of butter and finally the third, folding, pressing and rolling in between each batch. You will need to sprinkle both the work surface and the dough with flour as you work.

Finish by rolling and folding the dough without adding any butter. Press the edges at the side as before to seal. Transfer the dough to a plate, cover with clingfilm and chill in the fridge for 30 minutes.

Sprinkle the work surface with flour. Roll out the dough as before and repeat the folding process 3 more times without adding butter. By this time you will have folded the dough 7 times and created lovely layers. Transfer to the plate, cover with clingfilm and chill for 45 minutes.

Take the dough out of the fridge and place it on a lightly floured work surface, with 1 of the folded sides to your right. Roll the dough out into a 60 x 30cm rectangle. Trim the sides, taking care not to drag the edges. Cut the rectangle in half straight through the middle and then each side into 7 evenly-sized rectangles. You should end up with 14 rectangles in total. Each rectangle should measure roughly 15 x 8.5cm. If your work surface isn't large enough to roll the dough out fully, cut it in half.

Take a rectangle and put a small amount of the chocolate in 2 lines, running 2cm in from each short side. Roll the dough inwards from both short sides, folding it over the chocolate to meet in the middle. Turn the pastry over and place it on the baking tray. Make each pain au chocolat in exactly the same way.

To make the glaze, whisk the egg with the caster sugar until smooth. Brush lightly over the pastries. Leave in a warm place for 20 minutes until lightly puffed up. Preheat the oven to 220°C/Fan 200°C/Gas 7. Brush the pastries once more with the glaze and bake in the centre of the oven for 15–18 minutes until risen and golden brown. Serve warm.

PAIN AUX RAISINS

Makes about 6 or 7

Another variation on the croissant, these are spiral-shaped goodies filled with raisins and marzipan. Freshly baked, they are complete heaven and well worth losing your waistline for.

BASIC DOUGH
1 tsp caster sugar
225ml warm water
1 x 7g sachet of fast-action dried yeast
450g strong white flour, plus extra for dusting
25g butter
1 medium egg

FILLING
200g raisins
225g butter
200g white marzipan, chilled

GLAZE
1 medium egg
1 tbsp caster sugar

Put the raisins for the filling in a bowl and pour over enough just-boiled water to cover. Leave them to soak and swell. Make the basic dough in the same way as for pain au chocolat (see page 196), following the instructions to the point where you have a rectangle of dough, measuring 60 x 30cm. Trim the sides, taking care not to drag the edges. If your work surface isn't large enough to roll the dough out fully, cut it in half before rolling.

Drain the raisins and scatter them over the dough. Grate the marzipan coarsely on top – taking care not to grate your fingers! Starting from one short edge, roll up the dough carefully and fairly firmly. Cut the dough at 2cm intervals with a sharp knife to form individual pastries. Place these on a large baking sheet, lined with baking parchment, with the filling facing upwards and press down very lightly.

To make the glaze, whisk the egg with the caster sugar and brush lightly over the pastries. Leave in a warm place for about 20 minutes. Preheat the oven to 220°C/Fan 200°C/Gas 7. Brush the pastries with the glaze once more and bake them in the centre of the oven for 12–15 minutes or until well risen and golden brown. Serve warm.

MADELEINES

Makes 12

These are exquisitely sophisticated little cakes that think they're biscuits. They are believed to have been first made in Commercy, a town in the Lorraine region of northern France and they're baked in special shell-shaped moulds. There's no better reason for bringing out your best china than for a freshly baked batch of madeleines.

50g butter	1 tsp vanilla extract
1 large egg	50g plain flour, sifted
50g caster sugar	icing sugar, sifted, to decorate

Preheat the oven to 190°C/Fan 170°C/Gas 5. Gently melt the butter in a small saucepan. Using a pastry brush, grease the madeleine moulds with a little of the melted butter. Set the rest of the melted butter aside.

Beat the egg, caster sugar and vanilla extract with an electric hand-whisk until the mixture is very pale and thick and the beaters leave a visible trail when lifted from the bowl. Sift the flour into the bowl and gently fold it into the beaten egg mixture with a large metal spoon. Pour in the rest of the melted butter around the edge of the batter and fold it in very gently.

Spoon some cake batter into each madeleine mould and bake for 8–10 minutes until the little cakes are well risen and pale golden brown. Leave them to cool in the tin for 5 minutes, then turn them out on to a wire rack. Dust with icing sugar once cool.

CHOCOLATE & ORANGE SOUFFLÉS

The French word 'soufflé' means 'puffed up' which is exactly what a good soufflé should be. Soufflés were invented in France in the 18th century and have been a classic of French cuisine ever since. There are sweet and savoury versions, but we think you can't beat a chocolate soufflé.

15g butter, for greasing
brown sugar, for sprinkling
150g dark chocolate, broken into squares
3 large egg yolks
75ml double cream
finely grated zest of ½ small orange
2 tbsp orange liqueur, such as Cointreau
½ tsp vanilla extract

5 large egg whites
40g soft light brown sugar
icing sugar and finely grated orange zest, to decorate

BOOZY CREAM
200ml double cream
2 tbsp orange liqueur, such as Cointreau
2 tbsp soft light brown sugar

Grease 6 x 175ml large ramekins or large ovenproof coffee cups with butter. Sprinkle a little brown sugar in each ramekin or cup and roll it around until the inside is lightly coated in sugar. Place the ramekins or cups on a baking tray, spaced well apart.

Put the chocolate in a heatproof bowl and set it over a pan of gently simmering water. Melt over a low heat until almost smooth, then carefully remove the bowl and stir the chocolate with a wooden spoon until smooth. Beat the 3 egg yolks into the hot melted chocolate and stir in the cream, zest, liqueur and vanilla extract. Leave to cool for 10 minutes. Preheat the oven 220°C/ Fan 200°C/Gas 7.

While the chocolate mixture is cooling, prepare the boozy cream. Put the double cream, liqueur and sugar in a mixing bowl and whip with an electric whisk until soft peaks form. Set aside.

Whisk the 5 egg whites together in a large bowl until stiff but not dry. You should be able to turn the bowl upside down without the egg whites sliding out. Add the 40g of soft brown sugar, a little at a time, whisking well in between each addition.

Fold a quarter of the egg whites into the chocolate mixture to loosen it, then fold in the rest with a metal spoon. Take care not to over stir the mixture or the eggs will lose volume. If you have some stubborn lumps of egg white, cut through the mixture a couple of times with a large metal whisk instead of folding or stirring.

Spoon the mixture into the ramekins and bake in the centre of the oven for about 9–10 minutes until well risen but with a slight wobble in the centre. Dust the tops with sifted icing sugar, place the ramekins on dessert plates and top with spoonfuls of boozy cream. Sprinkle with a little orange zest and serve immediately.

RASPBERRY & PEACH JALOUSIE

Serves 6

A jalousie is a fruit-filled pastry dessert, with the top slashed at intervals so that the filling shows through. This pud gets its curious name because it is thought to look a bit like a sort of slatted louvre window that's called – guess what? – a jalousie!

500g puff pastry	100g blackcurrants or blueberries
plain flour, for dusting	75g caster sugar, plus 2 tsp
2 ripe but firm peaches	2 tbsp cornflour
150g raspberries	1 medium egg white, beaten

Preheat the oven to 220°C/Fan 200°C/Gas 7. Line a large baking sheet with baking parchment. Roll the pastry out on a lightly floured surface to make a 36cm square, then cut it in half to make 2 rectangles and place 1 rectangle on the baking sheet.

Take a peach and, using a small knife, carefully cut towards the stone from the stalk to the base. Move the peach around in your hand and make another cut towards the stone in exactly the same way to create a slice from the peach. Flip the slice out into a bowl.

Continue working around the peach until you have cut about 12 slices and you are left holding an almost completely clean stone. Hold the peach with a clean tea towel, if you like, to protect your hand. Slice the other peach in the same way.

Toss the peach slices with the raspberries and blackcurrants or blueberries, 75g caster sugar and cornflour until all the fruit is evenly coated. Arrange the fruit down the centre of the pastry, leaving a 6cm border at each end and 4cm on each long side. Put the egg white in a small bowl and stir vigorously with a pastry brush until frothy, then brush it over the pastry border around the fruit.

Place the second rectangle of pastry on the work surface. Fold the pastry in half lengthwise without pressing it down. Starting roughly 6cm in from one end, make 9 cuts of 5cm across the folded pastry through both layers, leaving a 4cm border around the edge. Open out the pastry and place it over the fruit. Press the pastry edges firmly to seal and trim the edges neatly, trying not to drag the pastry as it will affect the rise. Brush the pastry with a little more egg white and sprinkle with the 2 teaspoons of caster sugar. Bake in the centre of the oven for about 25 minutes or until the pastry is well risen and golden brown. Serve warm.

pain de
campagne
1€90

PEAR & WALNUT FRANGIPANE TART

Serves 8

Frangipane is a sweet pastry cream, usually used as a base for fruit in tarts. It is generally made with almonds, but we have used walnuts for our version. Frangipane was first mentioned in a French cookery book in 1674 and has been around ever since. This is a really posh-looking dish and you'll be proud to bring it to the table.

150g walnuts
175g softened butter
175g golden caster sugar
75g self-raising flour
2 medium eggs, beaten
½ tsp vanilla extract
3 ripe but firm Conference pears

2 tbsp fresh lemon juice

PASTRY
250g plain flour, plus extra for dusting
150g cold butter, cut into cubes
1 tbsp caster sugar
1 large egg, beaten

Preheat the oven 200°C/Fan 180°C/Gas 6. To make the pastry, put the flour, butter and sugar in a food processor and blend until the mixture resembles fine breadcrumbs. With the motor running, slowly add the egg to the flour mixture. Turn off the motor as soon as the dough forms a ball.

Roll out the pastry on a well-floured surface, lifting and turning after every few rolls, and use it to line a loose-based, fluted 25cm tart tin. If the pastry tears a little, repair any gaps with the trimmings. Pinch off the excess pastry with your thumb and forefinger, leaving 2–3mm above the top of the tin to help compensate for any shrinkage.

Line the pastry case with crumpled baking parchment and half fill with baking beans. Bake for 25 minutes, then remove the paper and beans and cook for a further 5 minutes. Set the pastry aside while you make the filling. Reduce the oven temperature to 180°C/Fan 160°C/ Gas 4.

Put 100g of the walnuts in a food processor and blitz to fine crumbs. Add the butter, sugar, flour, eggs and vanilla, then blend well. Spread the walnut mixture evenly over the cooled pastry case, starting at the edge before heading into the centre.

Peel the pears and cut them in half. Remove the cores, put the pear halves into a large bowl and toss with the lemon juice to prevent them turning brown. One at a time, place each pear half on a board and cut it into slices, starting at the short end. Carefully transfer the pear slices to the tart case and press them into the frangipane, short end towards the middle. Repeat with the remaining pears. Dot with the reserved walnuts, broken in half if necessary.

Put the tart tin on a baking tray and bake in the centre of the oven for 50–60 minutes or until the pears are tender and the frangipane filling is well risen and golden brown. Leave the tart to stand for 15 minutes before lifting it from the tin and serve warm or cold.

NORMANDY APPLE TART
(Tarte aux pommes à la Normande)

Serves 8

A regular French apple tart has a base of apple purée under the apple slices, but the Normandy version has a creamy almond and Calvados filling. Every Normandy family has its own recipe, but this is ours – a proper homage to the apple.

3 eating apples, such as Cox, (about 450g unprepared weight)
1 x 350g Bramley cooking apple
3 large eggs
300g crème fraiche
125g caster sugar
3 tbsp Calvados or brandy

1 tsp ground cinnamon
1–2 tsp icing sugar, sifted, to decorate

PASTRY
250g plain flour, plus extra for dusting
150g cold butter, cut into cubes
2 tbsp caster sugar
1 large free-range egg, beaten

Preheat the oven to 200°C/Fan 180°C/Gas 6. To make the pastry, put the flour, butter and sugar in a food processor and blend until the mixture resembles breadcrumbs. With the motor running, slowly add the egg. Turn off the motor as soon as the dough forms a ball.

Roll out the pastry on a floured surface, lifting and turning after every few rolls, and use it to line a loose-based, fluted 25cm tart tin. If the pastry tears a little, repair any gaps with the trimmings. Pinch off the excess pastry with your thumb and forefinger, leaving 2–3mm above the top of the tin to help compensate for any shrinkage.

Line the pastry case with crumpled baking parchment and half fill with baking beans. Bake for 25 minutes, then remove the paper and beans and cook for a further 5 minutes. Set the pastry aside while you prepare the filling. Reduce the oven temperature to 180°C/Fan 160°C/ Gas 4.

Peel the apples, cut them into quarters and take out the cores, then cut into 2cm chunks. Scatter the apple pieces into the pastry case.

Beat the eggs in a large bowl with a metal whisk, then beat in the crème fraiche, sugar, Calvados and cinnamon until smooth. Pour this mixture over the apples and leave to stand for 2–3 minutes so that the mixture can seep down between the fruit pieces.

Bake on a baking tray in the centre of the oven for 40–45 minutes or until the apples are tender and the filling is set and pale golden brown. Check the apples by poking them with the tip of a small knife – it should slide in easily. Leave the tart to cool in the tin, then carefully slide it on to a plate. Dust with sifted icing sugar and serve with cream or ice cream.

BRIOCHE AUX PRALINES

Serves 10–12

Brioche is a rich yeast bread that contains lots of butter and eggs. Some say it was first made in Brittany, while others claim it is from Normandy, but it has been baked in Paris since the 17th century. The pink pralines (see page 227) make this extra special.

1 x 7g sachet of fast-action dried yeast
1 tsp caster sugar
125ml warm milk
500g plain flour, plus 50g extra for kneading
1 tsp fine sea salt

2 tbsp caster sugar, plus 1 tsp for sprinkling
4 medium eggs, beaten
175g butter, softened
sunflower oil, for greasing
75g pink (rose) pralines
1 egg yolk, beaten, to glaze

To make the dough, sprinkle the yeast and caster sugar on to the warm milk in a small bowl. Whisk lightly, then leave in a warm place for 10 minutes or until a light foam forms on the surface. Sift the flour, salt and caster sugar into a large mixing bowl. Make a well in the centre and pour in the yeast mixture and beaten eggs. Mix with a wooden spoon until it forms a ball.

Turn the dough out on to a floured surface and knead it gently for about 5 minutes until smooth. Gradually add the softened butter, a teaspoon at a time, kneading well in between each addition. It will take about 10 minutes to incorporate the butter and the dough will be sticky. Flour the surface generously as you knead in the butter.

On a clean floured surface and using clean hands, sprinkle the dough with more flour. Continue to knead lightly for a further 10 minutes or until the dough is very pliable, smooth and slightly shiny but no longer sticky. Place the dough in a large lightly oiled bowl and cover with oiled clingfilm. Leave in a warm place for 1½ hours until well risen and spongy.

Put the pralines a few at a time in a pestle and mortar and crush them roughly. Some will become powdery but you should have some larger chunks too. Tip them into a bowl as soon as each batch is done. Set aside.

Oil a 23cm spring-clip cake tin and line the base with baking parchment. Turn the dough out on to a lightly floured surface and knock it back with your knuckles. Knead for a minute or so, then roll it out with a floured rolling pin to make a square measuring 35 x 35cm.

Sprinkle the crushed pralines over the top, taking them all the way to the edge. Roll the dough up like a Swiss roll and cut it into 4cm slices with a sharp knife. Arrange the slices in the tin, placing them cut-side up. They should fit fairly snuggly. Cover the tin loosely with oiled clingfilm and leave in a warm place for about 45 minutes or until the dough is well risen.

Preheat the oven 180°C/Fan 160°C/Gas 4. Bake the brioche for 30 minutes, then remove it from the oven and brush lightly but generously with the beaten egg yolk. Return the brioche to the oven for a further 10 minutes until golden brown. Cool in the tin for 10 minutes, then release on to a wire rack. Sprinkle with sugar and serve warm or cold.

FLAN DE SAINT-JEAN-DE-MINERVOIS

Serves 8–10

If you like crème caramel you're going to love this – a version fit for an emperor. It's made with a very special sweet wine from the South of France called Muscat de Saint-Jean-de-Minervois. If you don't want to use wine, you can use an extra 100ml of milk.

CARAMEL
100g granulated sugar
2 tbsp water

CUSTARD
900ml whole milk

4 tbsp lavender honey
finely grated zest of 1 orange
9 large eggs
100ml sweet muscat wine
(or any other dessert wine)

To make the caramel, heat the sugar and water in a heavy-based pan until the sugar dissolves, stirring occasionally. Once the sugar has dissolved, stop stirring and cook until the sugar syrup caramelises and turns a deep golden brown. Swirl the liquid in the pan occasionally so that it doesn't burn. As soon as the caramel is ready, pour it carefully into a 1.5 litre non-stick ridged flan tin. Holding the tin with an oven cloth, tip the caramel up into the ridges – be very careful as the caramel will be extremely hot! Leave to one side while the caramel sets.

To make the custard, pour the milk into a medium non-stick saucepan and add the honey and orange zest. Bring to a simmer and cook until the honey dissolves, stirring occasionally. Watch carefully so that it doesn't boil over. Remove the milk from the heat and leave to infuse for 10 minutes. Meanwhile, bring a kettle of water to the boil and preheat the oven to 170°C/Fan 150°C/Gas 3½. Put the flan tin into a roasting tin.

Whisk the eggs and wine together until pale and creamy. Strain the hot milk and honey through a fine sieve into a jug, then pour on to the eggs and wine, stirring constantly. Pour the custard into the flan tin on top of the caramel. Pour just-boiled water into the roasting tin to come halfway up the sides of the flan tin. This helps the custard cook gently and gives a smooth texture to the finished flan.

Bake for 45–50 minutes or until the custard is just set. Cover the tin loosely with foil halfway through the cooking time to prevent the top browning too much. The custard should still be fairly wobbly in the centre when it is cooked and will continue to set as it cools. Take the roasting tin out of the oven and leave the flan to cool in the water for at least an hour. Once cooled, cover with clingfilm and transfer to the fridge. Chill for at least 6 hours or overnight.

To serve, press the custard all the way around with your finger tip to break the seal at the edge of the tin. Place a fairly deep serving plate on top of the tin (to contain the caramel) and invert. Holding both the plate and flan tin tightly together, give a small shake. The custard should then drop down on to the plate. Pour any caramel in the dish over the custard. If the custard is reluctant to leave the tin, dip the base very quickly into a bowl of just-boiled water and try again. Serve with cream.

RASPBERRY MACAROONS
(Macarons framboise)

———

Makes 26 filled macaroons

When we were kids, a macaroon was a crunchy little biscuit made of chopped almonds, sugar and egg whites. Now there are much posher versions, known as French macaroons, which look – and taste – amazing and are sold in fancy shops. We've discovered that they are not difficult to make and the results are truly impressive. Raspberry and lemon (see page 218) are our favourites, but whatever the flavour, macaroons look delicate and beautiful.

1 tsp sunflower oil
3 large egg whites
a pinch of fine sea salt
50g caster sugar
pink food colouring paste
115g ground almonds
225g icing sugar

FILLING
100ml double cream
2 tbsp seedless raspberry jam,
   stirred well to soften
1 tsp rose water for cooking
pink food colouring paste

Grease 2 sturdy baking trays with oil and line them with baking parchment. The oil helps the paper stick.

Put the egg whites in a large mixing bowl, add the salt and whisk with electric beaters until stiff but not dry. Slowly whisk in the caster sugar, a teaspoon at a time. Using a cocktail stick, add small dabs of food colouring to the egg white, whisking well in between each addition. Make the colour a little stronger than you want in the final macaroons as it will fade during cooking.

Rub the ground almonds with your fingertips to break up any large lumps. Sift the icing sugar on top of the meringue, scatter with the ground almonds and fold in using a large metal spoon. Try to keep as much air as possible in the meringue while squishing out any bumps and lumps. The volume will reduce but this is normal.

Put the meringue in a piping bag fitted with a 1cm plain nozzle and pipe rounds of about 3cm across on to the baking trays. You'll find that the meringue will begin oozing out of the piping nozzle as you hold it vertically, so it's important to work quickly with a good downward pressure on the bag. You should be able to fit about 26 piped blobs on each tray. Space them apart as they do spread a little.

Dip your finger in a little water and gently flatten any tops that look too pointy. Give the trays a couple of taps on the work surface to help get rid of any large bubbles. Leave them to stand for 30–60 minutes to allow the meringue to set and help create a smooth, shiny crust. If you touch 1 of the macaroons lightly with your fingertip, it shouldn't feel wet or tacky. Leave for a little longer if it does.

Preheat the oven to 170°C/Fan 150°C/Gas 3½. Bake the macaroons, a tray at a time, on the middle shelf of the oven, for 9–10 minutes. The tops should be crisp and they should look slightly risen. Leave to cool on the baking trays.

To fill the macaroons, whip the cream with the raspberry jam, rose water and a little pink colouring until soft peaks form. Using a teaspoon, dab a little of the cream into the centre of 26 of the macaroons.

Top with the remaining macaroons and put them on a pretty serving plate or in a decorative box. Cover and store in the fridge for up to 2 days before eating, but ideally eat these the day that they are made.

Tip: Fill with a buttercream icing or white chocolate ganache if you prefer.

LEMON MACAROONS
(Macarons au citron)

Makes 26 filled macaroons

French macaroons, called 'macarons' in France, are said to have first been made
in a French convent in 1791. But some claim that the recipe was brought from Italy
by Catherine de Medici's chefs way back in 1533, when she came to France to marry
Henry II. The French macaroons we know and love today – neat little rounds that are
crisp on the outside, meltingly soft in the middle and sandwiched with buttercream –
were created by master baker Pierre Desfontaines of the Ladurée pastry shop in
Paris at the beginning of the 20th century.

1 tsp sunflower oil
3 large egg whites
a pinch of fine sea salt
50g caster sugar
a few drops of lemon essence (optional)
yellow food colouring paste

115g ground almonds
225g icing sugar

FILLING
100ml double cream
3 tbsp lemon curd

Make these in the same way as the raspberry macaroons on page 216, but add the lemon
essence, if using, to the egg whites and caster sugar before adding the food colouring.

To fill the macaroons, whip the cream with the lemon curd until soft peaks form. Spoon into a
piping bag fitted with a large plain nozzle and pipe into the centre of 26 of the macaroons. Top
with the remaining macaroons and put them on a pretty serving plate or in a decorative box.

Store the macaroons in the fridge for up to 2 days before eating, but ideally eat these on the day
that they are made.

PROVENÇAL BISCUITS
(Biscottes de Provence)

Makes about 16

France has always been famous for its cheese and these tasty little biscuits do it proud. They're good with some of our great British cheeses too.

100g plain flour, plus extra for dusting
100g wholemeal flour
1 tsp fine sea salt
½ tsp fennel seeds
1 tsp dried basil
1 tbsp finely chopped fresh rosemary leaves

1 tbsp finely chopped fresh thyme leaves
75g cold butter, cut into cubes
1 medium egg yolk
1 tsp Dijon mustard
3 tbsp cold water

Preheat the oven to 180°C/Fan 160°C/Gas 4. Line a baking tray with baking parchment. Put both flours in a large bowl and add the salt, fennel, basil, rosemary and thyme. Toss together until well combined, then add the butter.

Using your fingertips, rub the butter into the seasoned flour until the mixture resembles breadcrumbs, then make a well in the centre. Whisk the egg, mustard and water together in a bowl and pour the mixture on to the flour.

Using a round-bladed knife and then your hands, bring all the ingredients together to form a stiff dough. Press the dough into a rough ball. Turn the dough out on to a lightly floured surface and knead gently until pliable.

Roll out the pastry until it is about 3mm thick (the thickness of a £1 coin), turning and lifting it regularly so that it doesn't get a chance to stick. Sprinkle a little flour under the dough when you lift it.

Cut the dough into rounds with a 6.5cm plain or fluted cutter and place the rounds on the baking tray. Re-knead and roll the trimmings as required. Bake the biscuits in the centre of the oven for 20–25 minutes until they are firm and lightly browned. Cool on the baking tray, then store them in an airtight container. They should keep well for up to 5 days. Serve with some good cheese.

TRADITIONAL
FRENCH BAGUETTE

—

Makes 6

Bread is a serious business in France and the ingredients in a baguette are controlled by law. We went to see baguettes being made in a bakery in Carcassonne. It was just a normal neighbourhood place, but the bread they made was of fantastic quality and baked fresh four times a day– it's what people expect and demand. This is their recipe.

1kg strong plain flour, plus extra for dusting
1 tbsp dried yeast (not the fast-acting type)
½ tsp salt

500ml warm water
oil, for greasing

Tip the flour into a large mixing bowl. Sprinkle the salt over one half of the flour in the bowl and the yeast over the other half of the flour. Slowly add the water and, using your hands, mix to a soft dough. Turn the dough out on to a floured work surface and knead for at least 10 minutes. The dough should be very supple and elastic.

Place the dough in a lightly oiled mixing bowl. Cover with a clean tea towel and leave the dough to rest for 24 hours in a cool place, until it has doubled or tripled in size.

Turn the dough out on to a lightly floured surface and knock it back with your knuckles. Cut the dough into 6 pieces and shape each piece into a baguette, 35cm long.

Place directly on to a floured baking sheet or into a couche (a special canvas cloth for use with baguettes). For a makeshift couche, heavily flour 2 clean tea towels. Lay a baguette along the edge of 1 of the tea towels and pleat the tea towel up against the edge of the baguette. Place another baguette next to the pleats. Repeat the process until you have 6 baguettes lined up against each other with pleated tea towel in between each. The tea towel supports the sides and gives the baguettes a better shape as they rise. Cover the baguettes with a clean tea towel and leave in a cool place for 12 hours.

Preheat the oven to 240°C/Fan 220°C/Gas 9. Place a roasting tin on the bottom of the oven. Bring a kettle of water to the boil.

Gently roll the baguettes out of the tea towels on to a floured baking sheet. With a very sharp knife, cut 4 or 5 diagonal slits across the surface of the baguettes, then place them on the top shelf of the oven. Fill the roasting tin with boiling water from the kettle – be careful as the water will splutter as you pour it in. The boiling water creates steam in the oven which helps make the baguettes crusty. Bake them for 15–20 minutes until golden, then leave to cool on a wire rack before tearing into them!

PATRICIA'S CLAFOUTIS

Serves 8

The clafoutis comes from Limousin in central France. It is basically a baked custard, traditionally made with cherries but any fruit can be used. This is a special gluten-free version – some recipes include flour – that we got from Dave's old friend Patricia, who we met up with in the South of France. They used to share a flat when they were students and hadn't seen each other for 30 years or more. It was a wonderful reunion and she treated us to this great clafoutis.

40g butter, melted, plus extra for greasing
600g seasonal fruits such as berries, cherries, or raspberries
200ml milk
100ml double cream

4 eggs
60g caster sugar
1 tsp vanilla extract
a pinch of salt
icing sugar for dusting

Preheat the oven to 220°C/Fan 200°C/Gas 7. Grease a 23cm ovenproof flan dish with butter. Wash and prepare the fruit as necessary, removing stalks and stones, then scatter the fruit over the base of the flan dish.

Pour the melted butter into a large bowl with the milk and double cream. Add the eggs, caster sugar, vanilla extract and salt and whisk together until combined.

Pour the batter over the fruit, place in the oven and cook for 10 minutes. Turn the oven down to 180°C/Fan 160°C/Gas 4 and cook for another 20 minutes. Remove the clafoutis from the oven and dust with icing sugar before serving hot or cold.

PINK PRALINE TART

Serves 6

Pink pralines are speciality of Lyon and a fashionable ingredient at the moment. They are simply chopped almonds with a pink sugar coating and they taste fab. You can buy them in some delis and chocolate shops or look for an online supplier – they last for ages. We ate this tart in a posh bakery and cake shop in Lyon, one of the gastronomic centres of Europe, and they gave us the recipe. Pâte sablée is a rich crumbly pastry.

PÂTE SABLÉE	250g flour, plus extra for dusting
1 medium egg	finely grated zest of 1 lemon
120g butter	
125g caster sugar	**TOPPING**
a pinch of salt	250g pink pralines, lightly crushed
	250ml crème fraiche

Put the egg, butter, sugar and salt in a food processor and whiz until pale and fluffy. Carefully add the flour and process again until the mixture resembles breadcrumbs, then add the lemon zest. Tip the mixture out on to the work surface and bring it together with your hands to form a ball. Wrap the pastry in clingfilm and leave it to rest for at least an hour before rolling it out.

Preheat the oven to 180°C/Fan 160°C/ Gas 4. Roll the pastry out on a floured surface and use it to line a 23cm tart tin. Prick the pastry, then cover it with crumpled baking parchment and baking beans and bake it for 20 minutes. Take it out of the oven, remove the beans and the greaseproof paper and bake for a further 5 minutes or until golden.

Leave the pastry case to cool in the tin while you make the topping. Pour the crème fraiche into a saucepan and add the crushed pralines. Cook over a medium heat, stirring constantly until the mixture reaches exactly 121°C – check with a sugar thermometer.

It's crucial that the mixture reaches this temperature. If it's not hot enough it won't set. If it's too hot it will be inedibly hard! Once the mixture has reached the right temperature, pour it into the pre-cooked pastry case and leave to cool.

Serve the pink praline tart in small slices – it's really very rich!

SPAIN

We travelled to the real
Spain for a taste of some
of the best country food,
such as Basque chicken
pie and rustic bread. It
was a million miles away
from the costas and the
tourists – and a real fiesta
for the senses.

BASQUE CHICKEN PIE
(Oilasko pastela)

Serves 4–5

Some say that Basque food is the best in Spain and if this top-notch pie is anything to go by, they're right! This is like having a flamenco danced on your tongue.

4 boneless, skinless chicken thighs, cut into bite-sized pieces
2 tsp smoked paprika
2 tsp flaked sea salt
2 tbsp olive oil
2 medium onions, cut into 12 wedges
1 green pepper, halved, seeded and sliced
1 red pepper, halved, seeded and sliced
3–4 sprigs of fresh thyme
2 bay leaves
150g chorizo sausage, skinned and cut into thin slices
3 garlic cloves, crushed

4 large ripe tomatoes (each about 100g), skinned and roughly chopped
2 tbsp flour
freshly ground black pepper

PASTRY
225g plain flour, plus extra for dusting
1 tsp baking powder
½ tsp fine sea salt
75g unsalted butter, plus extra for greasing
1 medium egg yolk
4–5 tbsp cold water
1 egg, beaten, or whole milk, to glaze

Put the chicken pieces in a bowl and sprinkle over the paprika, salt and plenty of pepper. Rub the seasoning into the meat and set aside.

Heat the oil in a large frying pan and fry the onions and peppers with the thyme and bay leaves for 3 minutes, while stirring. Add the chicken and seasoning and cook for another 3 minutes, turning the chicken regularly until it is starting to colour. Add the chorizo and garlic and fry for 2 minutes more. Add the tomatoes and cook for 5 minutes or until they are softened and juicy, stirring regularly.

Tilt the pan so that the liquid runs to one side and sprinkle the flour over the vegetables, chicken and chorizo. Stir it in quickly, then set the pan level and stir the cooking liquor into the flour. Doing it this way should prevent little clumps of flour – but don't worry if you do have a few, no one will notice. Add more salt and pepper if necessary and continue to cook for 1 minute, stirring until the sauce thickens. Remove from the heat and tip everything into a roasting tin or ovenproof dish, measuring about 25 x 30cm and at least 4cm deep. Leave to cool.

For the pastry, pulse the flour, baking powder, salt, butter and egg yolk in a food processor until the mixture resembles breadcrumbs. Slowly pour in the water with the motor running, blending until the mixture just comes together as a dough. (You may not need to use all of the water.) Form the dough into a ball. Preheat the oven to 200°C/Fan 180°C/Gas 6.

Roll the pastry out into a rectangle about the same size as the tin. Place it over the pie filling and tuck the sides of the pastry down around the filling. Brush with beaten egg or milk to glaze. Bake for about 30 minutes or until the pastry is golden and the filling is hot.

GALICIAN PIE
(Empanada Gallega)

Serves 6

These super Spanish pies – empanadas – can be stuffed with whatever seasonal fillings you like and made as one big pie as we've done here, or several smaller ones. You can make special empanada pastry, but we've used our own in our version of this recipe.

PASTRY
250g plain flour, plus extra for dusting
a good pinch of fine sea salt
1 tsp baking powder
4 tbsp olive oil, plus extra for greasing
1 medium egg, beaten
125ml water
1 egg, beaten, to seal and glaze

FILLING
2 tbsp olive oil
1 large onion, finely diced
1 green pepper, halved, seeded
  and cut into thin strips
1 red pepper, halved, seeded
  and cut into thin strips
150g shelled scallops, patted dry
  with kitchen paper and cut into 5mm strips
200g thickly sliced cooked ham,
  cut into 1cm cubes
4 tbsp chopped fresh flat-leaf parsley
freshly squeezed juice of 1 lemon
1 tsp fine sea salt
½ tsp coarsely ground black pepper

To make the pastry, place the flour, salt and baking powder in a bowl and make a well in the centre. Add the oil and beaten egg and gradually incorporate the flour into the liquid. Start adding the water a little at a time until the mixture forms a slightly sticky (but not wet) and elastic dough. (You may not need all the water depending on the size of the egg you are using.) Bring the dough together with your hands. Put it on a plate, sprinkle with a little flour, cover with clingfilm and chill in the fridge for 30–60 minutes.

To make the filling, heat the oil in a frying pan and fry the onion until soft but not coloured, stirring regularly. Add the peppers and cook for 3 minutes, stirring, then add the scallops and fry for 30 seconds, stirring constantly. Take the pan off the heat, quickly add the ham, parsley, lemon juice, salt and pepper and mix everything together. Leave to cool for 20–30 minutes.

Preheat the oven to 200°C/Fan 180°C/Gas 6. Weigh the pastry and divide the weight by 5. Roll two-fifths of the pastry into a ball and put it to one side. Form the rest into a slightly larger ball. Roll out the larger ball of pastry until it forms a circle about the size of a dinner plate and place it on a lightly oiled baking sheet. Spoon the cooled filling into the centre of the pastry and spread it out towards the edge, leaving a 2cm border all the way around. Brush the border lightly with beaten egg.

Roll out the remaining pastry slightly smaller than the base of the pie and gently place it over the filling. Bring the base up to meet the smaller pastry disc and fold it over, pressing and crimping into a rope shape to make a sealed pastry edge.

Brush the pastry with beaten egg and make a couple of small slits in the top to allow the steam to escape. Bake in the centre of the oven for 20–25 minutes until the pastry is golden brown and the filling is hot. Serve warm or cold.

SPANISH BREAD
(Pan de horno)

Makes 8

Good Spanish bread is served with everything from tapas to tortillas. This version is seasoned with olives to make it extra tasty and is great for lunchtime rolls, filled with Serrano ham and Manchego cheese.

1 tsp caster sugar
250ml warm water
1 x 7g sachet of fast-action dried yeast
450g strong white flour, plus extra for dusting

2 tsp fine sea salt
3 tbsp virgin olive oil, plus extra for greasing
100g pitted green or black olives,
  roughly chopped

Whisk together the sugar and warm water in a medium bowl. Stir in the yeast very lightly, then set aside in a warm place for about 10 minutes or until you see a beige foam floating on the surface.

Mix the flour and salt together in a large bowl and make a well in the centre. Gradually pour in the foamy liquid and bring the dough together, using clean hands. It is a slightly drier dough than other breads, so you will need to work hard. Just as you are getting there, gradually start adding the oil and it will start to ease a little.

Tip the stiff dough on to a work surface and knead for 10 minutes until it feels smooth and more elastic. You may need to use a little flour to prevent it becoming too sticky, but try to avoid adding too much as it could make the dough very dry. Place the dough in a lightly oiled bowl, cover with lightly oiled clingfilm and leave it in a warm place for about an hour or until well risen.

Turn the dough out on to the work surface again and shape it gently into a flattened ball. Sprinkle the chopped olives into the centre and knead them gently into the dough. Divide the dough into 8 even portions. Form each portion into a slightly oval shape by pulling the dough from the sides into the middle, pinching them together and then turning the dough over. Place each roll on a large, lightly greased baking tray as soon as it is made.

Using scissors, snip each roll twice to create a decorated top. Cover loosely with oiled clingfilm and leave the rolls to prove in a warm place for 45 minutes or until well risen.

Preheat the oven to 220°C/Fan 200°C/Gas 7. Bake the rolls for 15–20 minutes or until lightly browned. The bread should sound hollow when tapped on the base. Cool on a wire rack.

RUSTIC SPANISH BREAD
(Pan rústico)

—

Makes 1 large loaf

The Spanish love their bread and after tasting this, so do we! With the starter mix, it's halfway to a sourdough and it's a good old-fashioned hearty bread that keeps well.

STARTER DOUGH
150ml warm water
1 tsp caster sugar
3 tsp fast-action dried yeast
125g strong white bread flour

BREAD DOUGH
200ml warm water

1 tsp caster sugar
1 tsp fast-action dried yeast
225g strong plain flour,
    plus extra for dusting
100g strong wholemeal flour
1 tsp salt
1 tbsp olive oil, plus extra for greasing

Pour the water into a medium bowl and stir in the sugar. Lightly stir in the yeast and leave in a warm place for about 10 minutes or until a beige foam floats on the surface. Stir in the flour to make a thick paste, then cover with clingfilm and leave at room temperature for 24 hours. At the end of the 24 hours the paste will smell yeasty and slightly fermented – a bit like beer.

For the bread dough, pour the water into a medium bowl and stir in the sugar. Lightly stir in the yeast and leave in a warm place for about 10 minutes or until a beige foam floats on the surface. Stir the flours and salt together in a large bowl, then make a well in the centre and add the starter dough, the oil and the recently made yeast and water mixture. Mix with a wooden spoon and then your hands until the mixture comes together and forms a slightly lumpy and sticky dough. If the dough feels a little dry, add another tablespoon or 2 of water.

Transfer the dough to a work surface and knead for a good 10 minutes until it's smooth and elastic. As you knead, push the dough away from you with the heel of your hand to stretch it as long as possible, then fold it back towards you. This will help strengthen the flour and trap air bubbles inside the loaf. Resist the temptation to add too much extra flour as it could make the dough dry. You should feel the dough change in texture as you work, so don't be afraid to be fairly robust with your stretching and folding. Put the dough in an oiled mixing bowl, cover it loosely with oiled clingfilm and leave it to rise for about an hour or until it has doubled in size.

Loosen the dough with a spatula and tip it on to a baking tray that you have lined with baking parchment and dusted with flour. Stretch the dough very gently until it's about 30cm long, then fold it in half and stretch again. Do the same thing twice more. This should help to give the dough a more holey texture. After the third stretch, shape the dough into a long loaf shape and slash the top a few times with a sharp knife. Dust with a little flour and leave to prove in a warm place for 45–60 minutes or until it has risen again and feels light and puffy. Preheat the oven to 240°C/Fan 220°C/Gas 8 and bake the loaf for 20–25 minutes or until golden brown and crusty. The base should sound hollow when tapped. Cool on a wire rack.

SPANISH CARAMEL CUSTARDS
(Flan)

Makes 6

You see this dish on every menu in Spain because people are passionate about it – and we are no exception. It's simple but so good.

CARAMEL
100g granulated sugar
2 tbsp water

CUSTARD
450ml full-fat milk

1 cinnamon stick
2 large eggs
2 large egg yolks
75g caster sugar
1 tsp pure vanilla extract

To make the caramel, place the sugar and water in a heavy-based saucepan and cook over a medium heat until the sugar dissolves, stirring occasionally. Stop stirring and continue to cook until the sugar syrup caramelises and turns a deep golden brown. Swirl the liquid in the pan occasionally so that it doesn't burn and don't overcook or the caramel could become bitter. As soon as the caramel is ready, carefully pour it into 6 ramekin dishes and set them aside while the caramel sets.

To make the custard, pour the milk into a non-stick saucepan, add the cinnamon stick and bring to a simmer. Don't let it boil over. Remove the pan from the heat and leave the milk to infuse for 10 minutes. Meanwhile, bring a kettle of water to the boil, preheat the oven to 150°C/ Fan 130°C/Gas 2 and put the ramekins in a small roasting tin.

Whisk the eggs and egg yolks with the sugar and vanilla until pale and creamy. Remove the cinnamon stick and pour the hot milk over the eggs and sugar, whisking constantly until combined. Strain the custard through a fine sieve into a jug and then carefully pour it into the ramekins on top of the caramel.

Pour the just-boiled water from the kettle into the roasting tin until it comes three-quarters of the way up the sides of the ramekins. Lift the tin carefully into the oven and bake the custards for 40 minutes or until they are just set.

Take the tin out of the oven and, using an oven glove, take the ramekins out of the water and leave them to cool for at least an hour. Once cooled, cover the ramekins with clingfilm and put them in the fridge for at least 4 hours or overnight.

To serve, place a small plate on top of a ramekin and invert. Holding both the plate and ramekin tightly together, give a firm shake. The custard should drop down on to the plate. Pour any caramel in the dish over the custard and repeat the method with the remaining ramekins. If the custards are reluctant to leave the dishes, dip the base of each ramekin into a bowl of just-boiled water and try again.

CASA JULIAN ®

ALMOND COOKIES
(Polverones)

Makes about 12

Almonds are a much-loved ingredient in Spain and these little almond cookies are a traditional Christmas treat. They have a deliciously soft, crumbly texture – the Spanish name comes from the word 'polvo', which means dust.

75g icing sugar, plus extra for dusting
250g plain flour
75g ground almonds
a good pinch of fine sea salt
125g butter, softened
(or half lard and half butter)

Sift the icing sugar and flour into a bowl and stir in the ground almonds and salt. Add the softened butter and very slowly rub all the fat into the dry ingredients with your fingertips. It will take a short while and feel quite dry to begin with, but as you continue working, the ingredients will begin to form a dough – similar to a good shortbread mixture.

Preheat the oven to 180°C/Fan 160°C/Gas 4. Line a large baking tray with baking parchment. As soon as the dough begins to come together, form it into a flattened ball and place between 2 sheets of baking parchment. It will be very crumbly, so you may need to press it together a little. Press the dough down very gently with a rolling pin until it is about 2cm thick.

Cut the dough into rounds using a small plain 4–5cm biscuit cutter and transfer them to the lined tray with a palette knife. Bring the trimmings together and place them between the baking parchment sheets. Press and cut the dough into more rounds and put these on the tray. Bake the biscuits for 12–15 minutes or until firm and just beginning to turn golden. They should look pale, so don't let them brown too much.

Cool on the tray – don't forget, they will be rather crumbly. Dust with icing sugar to serve. These biscuits will keep very well in an airtight tin for up to a week.

ST JAMES'S CAKE
(*Tarta de Santiago*)

Serves 10

This famous dessert is somewhere between a tart and a cake and is traditionally decorated with a cross on the top. It has pastry on the bottom in some recipes and the deliciously moist sponge filling is made with ground almonds instead of flour.

PASTRY	FILLING
100g cold butter, cut into cubes,	350g ground almonds
200g plain flour, plus extra for dusting	150g caster sugar
plus extra for greasing	finely grated zest of 1 large lemon
50g ground almonds	6 medium eggs
25g caster sugar	
1 medium egg yolk	**TO DECORATE**
1 tbsp cold water	1 tsp icing sugar

Butter a 24cm spring-clip cake tin and dust with a teaspoon of flour, rolling it around the tin until the inside is evenly and lightly coated. Tip out any excess.

To make the pastry, put the butter, flour, almonds and sugar into a food processor and pulse until the mixture resembles fine breadcrumbs. Beat the egg yolk and water together. Gradually add the beaten egg to the flour mixture with the motor running and pulse until it forms a ball. Wrap the pastry in clingfilm, flatten slightly and chill while the filling is prepared.

Preheat the oven to 190°C/Fan 170°C/Gas 5. To make the filling, mix the ground almonds, sugar and lemon zest in a large bowl. Add the eggs, 1 at a time, beating well with a wooden spoon after each addition. Set the mixture aside.

Roll out the pastry on a lightly floured surface into a circle measuring about 24cm in diameter and the thickness of a £1 coin. Place the cake tin on top of the pastry and cut around it with a sharp knife to make a perfect circle. Use the pastry to line the base of the tin.

Pour the filling on to the pastry base and tap the tin on the work surface to ensure that the mixture is level. Bake for 20–25 minutes until risen, firm to the touch and pale golden brown. Leave to cool in the tin, then slide a knife around the cake, release the sides of the tin and gently slide it on to a serving plate.

To decorate, cut out a cross or sword symbol in greaseproof paper and place it on the cake. Sift icing sugar over the cake, taking care to keep the paper template in place. Very carefully peel it away to reveal the design.

SPELT BREAD WITH CHORIZO & HAM
(Pan de espelta con chorizo y jamón)

———

Makes 1 loaf

Spelt is an ancient grain that has a delicious nutty flavour and spelt flour can be used to bake excellent bread. We visited the amazing Escanda bakery in Lena, Asturias, where spelt bread is something of a speciality. They grow their own spelt and grind the flour themselves, and they very kindly gave us this recipe.

450g wholegrain spelt flour, plus extra for dusting
2 tsp baking powder
1 x 7g sachet of fast-action yeast
1 tsp salt

300ml water
oil, for greasing
75g sliced chorizo or salami, torn into pieces
100g sliced ham, torn into pieces

Mix the flour, baking powder, yeast and salt in a large bowl. Make a well in the centre, then add the water and mix well. Tip the dough out on to a lightly floured work surface and knead it lightly for 1–2 minutes until the dough is smooth. Do not knead it too long, though, as the gluten in spelt is more fragile than that in wheat flour. Place the dough in a lightly oiled bowl, cover with oiled clingfilm or a clean tea towel and leave to rise for 1 hour until it has doubled in size.

Preheat the oven to 180°C/Fan 160°C/Gas 4. Knock back the dough, then place it on a lightly floured surface and roll out to make a rectangle measuring about 20 x 30cm. Cover the surface of the dough with the torn pieces of chorizo and ham.

Starting from the shorter (20cm) side of the rectangle, roll up the dough, like a swiss roll. Place the roll on a floured baking sheet, join side down. Cook for 45–50 minutes until the loaf is golden brown and sounds hollow when tapped underneath. Cool on a wire rack.

RECIPES

BISCUITS

BREAD & ROLLS

CAKES

INDEX

ACKNOWLEDGMENTS

We had the best time on our baking trip around Europe and writing this book. We'd like to thank everyone who has helped put it all together.

Thanks to the extraordinarily talented Kate Barr and Lucie Stericker, whose design talents never cease to amaze us; to Cristian Barnett and his assistant Roy Baron for the photographs which are just brilliant; to the lovely Sammy-Jo and her assistants Becca Watson and Nikki Morgan for making the food look so mouth-wateringly fabulous for Cristian to photograph; to Amanda Harris and Jinny Johnson for getting us organised, helping us with the words and being generally wonderful; and to our good friend Justine Pattison for all her help and advice on the recipes, and to her assistants, Jane Rushworth, Fran Brown, Jane Gwillim, Lauren Spicer, Lauren Brignell.

A big thank you too for all the production team on the Bakation series: home economist: Sammy-Jo Squire; executive producer: Gill Tierney; series producer: Oliver Clark; directors: Joanna Brame, Dan Slee, Richard Sharman, François Gandolfi; editors: Ant Smith, Andrew McKenzie, Simon Prentice, Stephen Killick, Tim Savage; dubbing mixer: Kate Davis; production team: Sarah Greene, Emily Rushmer, Alison Davy, Abby Ross; researchers: Ruth Davies; Leila Finikarides; Julia Krysiak; Joel Gore; Stewart Bywater; cameramen: Roger Laxon, Jon Boast; sound men: James Baker, Tim Pitot; runners: Tim Jones, Matt Smith, Avone Keene; KTM: Ross Walker.

And as always, huge thanks to our wonderful families, who cheerfully put up with being force fed cakes and other baked goods for months on end. You're all amazing.